Play happy

ANARCHY PIE

Dedicated to my North Star
Anne-Marie Gilbraith

James Gilbraith

Anarchy Pie
First published in Great Britain in 2023 by The Guild of Reason

Copyright James Gilbraith 2023
James Gilbraith asserts the moral right to be identified
as the author of this work
A CIP Catalogue record for this book is available from the British Library

ISBN 978-1-3999-5091-6
Art Direction and Typeset by Giles Cooke at www.gilescooke.com
Edited by Matthew McKeown

Chapter list
1 – A Penny a Bee
2 – King of Clubs
3 – Shortbread and Shortcomings
4 – Body Count
5 – Zeros to Hero's
6 – Naked Neon Fish Porn
7 – Tangled Up In Boo
8 – 50 Miles of Lies
9 – Cable Ties and Duct Tape
10 – Croutons In The Soup
11 – Easy Rhythms and Random Notes
12 – EA – EH?

Cover painting – Robots – By James Gilbraith

Books by the same author :
Terminal Chancer, Silver Seasons, Atlantic Salmon
Hooked On Hope

Links
www.terminalchancer.co.uk
www.lostandfounduk.uk

Podcast – Hooked On Hope – Recast
Instagram – boo_gilbraith & lostandfoundclitheroe

Suggested Seasoning

The Polyphonic Spree - Lithium
Toots and the Maytals - Reggae Got Soul
Kevin Morby - Valley
Julia Jacklin - Don't Know How To Keep Loving You
Barry Brown - Rich Man Poor Man
Sam Dees - Lonely For You Baby
Little Richard - Long Tall Sally
Baby Huey - Hard Times
The Fall - A Day In The Life
Orbital/Sleaford Mods - Dirty Rat
Harry J Allstars - Liquidator
Lana Del Ray - Video Games
Jaques Dutronc - Et moi, et moi,et moi
Joe Jackson - Is She Really Going Out With Him
Run the Jewels - Ooh la la
Pokey LaFarge - Get it Fore Its Gone
Spanky Wilson - Sunshine of Your Love
UNKLE Mark Lanegan ESKA - Looking For The Rain
Joy Lovejoy - In Orbit
Les Symapthics de Porto Novo - A Min We Vo Nou We
Nolan Porter - Keep on, Keeping On
Aldous Harding - The Barrel
Nina Simone - Ain't Got No / I Got Life

Introduction

Firstly, can I just say a massive thank you for buying this book. I write and publish these books independently, so I appreciate the support. Secondly, if you enjoy the read then please do rigorously tell others, as word of mouth is all I have.

The River Ribble is 90km long. It starts at the confluence of Gayle Beck and Batty Wife Beck at Ribblehead, North Yorkshire (many scholars consider this the worst bit). The river falls a total of 544m as it runs through Horton in Ribblesdale, Settle and Nappa, and then it enters the lush, green, sophisticated and cultured county of Lancashire (many scholars consider this paradise the best bit). The river continues its journey through the villages and towns of Sawley, Grindleton, Clitheroe, Ribchester and Preston, before going on to empty into the Irish Sea at Lytham. Lancashire is in the North West of England (many scholars believe this to be easily the best bit).

This book is a continuation of my two previous efforts, Terminal Chancer and Hooked On Hope. Many of the themes and characters remain the same, the tone is abstract and the focus is on my affection for fishing, friendship, the outdoors, music, living slow and laughter. Usually, I attempt to capture a full season on the river and life's bleary edges, but this time I have covered the two seasons post-lockdown.

Each day, I wake up and imagine that I'm shooting a movie. Most days, my movies don't warrant sharing, so here I present the twelve that do. Suggested Seasoning represents the soundtrack.

Sun rises, sun sets, with life in between.

It's never easy, but it's always entertaining.

James Gilbraith

1
A Penny a Bee

Spring 2021 felt euphorically good. Ignore the usual automatic natural optimism, nature's flowing cycle of rebirth, the slow-turning rhythms of internal body clocks and the longer spells of golden, energising daylight; this most famous spring of 2021 came armed with a thumping bass line and a beautiful bouquet of hope, as Covid went into retreat and twenty-five million of the most vulnerable were vaccinated. It smiled like a radiant, lustrous movie star at a glamorous red-carpet premier, resplendent in the hard-earned promise it meant to keep, that life could possibly return to normal; the normal we all had numbly taken for granted. Normal had been duly chinned, bound, gagged and slapped senseless. Normal was properly fucked up, left slumped, dizzy and babbling in a feckless, flustered fog, wondering what day it was.

This most famous spring of 2021 better not be bullshitting, I thought. This most famous spring of 2021 better be the real fucking deal.

Most years, I am more than ready to throw a fly at the roulette wheel that is the River Ribble and try to catch an Atlantic salmon. This year, though, those restless feelings had been intensely amplified; I needed it even more than I wanted it. This year, it was absolutely essential for my sanity that I be on the river searching for my reset button. The need to momentarily unsubscribe from the festering media avalanche carrying a chilling cargo of so-called urgent global grey realities was achingly acute. Global lockdown must have had the streaming service industry wanking into a sock. Not their own sock, either; your sock, while you paid them for the privilege. With your subscription fees, they were able to pump the bile dial all the way up to eleven; the tired cliche of the coke-fuelled executive could ring true in those commissioning programme meetings. That could be a reasonable excuse. The other option is more sinister: how do you programme for an unparalleled generation of numb and dumber? What gems there must have been on the rejection list, as bloated, rutting executives in hideous, sweaty feeding frenzies gorged themselves on content, unable to believe their unimaginable dumb luck at their target audience being literally held captive and virtually gavage-fed. Keep 'em welded to their phones, their mantra repeated for months on end. Keep 'em trapped, keep 'em scrolling. Keep 'em hungry, but keep 'em alive. They're no good to us dead. The dead don't earn. The dead don't subscribe.

As you may have already fathomed from my unusually pessimistic tone, I really needed to leave the house.

Springtime on my home river, the Ribble, is the highlight of my angling year for several reasons. Normally, I am replenished, rested and ready; carried by the current of ardour and a riffle of rejuvenation. It's the starting point of my annual circle. Many other anglers are stirring, too; tentatively emerging from their lockdown hidey holes, rubbing their squared eyes while blinking blindly in the sunshine, wondering what the hell just happened and why they so readily know the names Carole Baskin and Joe Exotic; all deliriously high on the clear burning scent of hope and the taste of pensive anticipation on their lips, armed with the two thousand new flies they dutifully set about tying as a way to stop themselves from blowing their own brains out all over the new garden furniture. Yes, spring fishing is an intoxicating state, induced by leaning on experience and engaging muscle memory, blended with the potent poetic promise of the potential prize: an encounter with a wild, fresh-run, gleaming Atlantic salmon.

For me, spring fishing is a refreshingly time-efficient affair, ably aided by lengthening daylight hours that can facilitate a series of hit-it-and-quit-it or splash-and-dash bursts at beats that match the conditions and offer a chance to briefly narrow the odds. It's not a complete hit and hope, Hail Mary situation, however, as knowing the best height of water for fishing each beat is paramount to eliminating time waste. Plus, my windows of opportunity must be incorporated into a working, parental day. The longest I can remain off radar and temporarily lose myself is approximately four hours before I'm reeled in by somebody, somewhere for something, so there has to be a method to any madness.

Hustle is always the key: keep your shit primed, locked and loaded. The plan must be a savagely abrupt straight line from A to B. There is no time to dither or bloviate about verbose strategies. My rods are always set up behind my front door, waders in the boot of the car. With water on (i.e., if the river is up and falling), I will fish the club beats on my doorstep here at Clitheroe. This is generally my preference, due to the fact that I can be on our Low Moor beat in ten minutes flat. Another necessary consideration is the social aspect; if I've had half a bottle of red wine and a space cake with Lamont while fishing, I can leave the car and gently wander the mile home in an insulated comfort bubble, accompanied by a favourable playlist and wearing a play-happy grin (picture Frankenstein's Monster stoned off his neck bolts). If the river has dropped off, I will venture downstream around ten miles to the Salmesbury area, which can occasionally (rarely) produce a fish four hours after high tide. However, having recently read a very persuasive article about the glories of the River Eden, I have now joined Carlisle Angling Association, granting me access to some cracking water. It's a two-hundred-mile round trip, and thus falls beyond the parameters of the above-mentioned splash and dash, despite my optimistic description of it as a 'short hop without an impact overlap' in explaining the logic to my wife Anne-Marie. What this means in plain English is that if I leave at 6am and return for 5pm, there is zero impact overlap on family duties. That is until I'm found fast asleep in a chair by six.

Impact Overlap, you heard it here first. Rest assured, it will appear in all the big Sunday lifestyle supplements within twelve months.

'Johnathon and Amanda have reduced their stress levels by wild swimming and forest bathing. Their impact overlap is nearly always nil,' said Pascal, the couple's professional well-being coach, who is also developing their new three-acre property just outside Donostia, San Sebastian, in northern Spain.

During April, I raced the 'short hop' up to Carlisle, eager to get among some fresh fish, but after the third of these two-hundred-mile journeys and subsequent fifteen hours of casting, I was yet to get a pull. On that third visit, a dog-walking local informed me from the socially-safe distance of the far bank that I was too early – his point emphasised by dramatic head shaking, arm waving and mouthing of the words – before suggesting that I focus on the last two weeks of May instead. I treated this information with a great deal of suspicion, knowing that it could very easily have been a ploy to misdirect and keep invaders at bay. At the same time, I couldn't deny the fact that I hadn't seen a single fish.

If nothing else, those three sessions proved I was still keen as mustard. I'd fished in the freezing cold and endured some demoralising heavy rain, but the reality was that after much hype and an application process that amounted to a very mild form of interrogation, the Eden had left me decidedly underwhelmed (more on this in the chapter Naked Neon Fish Porn). Perhaps the experience suffered as a result of my lingering sense of punch-drunk, vacant confusion at this new post-Covid world. I still felt slightly off balance with it all, as I waded through the constant noise of fact, fiction, post-truth, new truth and fake news. I was maintaining and functioning, but with a fevered kind of neo-bewilderment.

Tip: if you, too, are feeling the cold, harsh bite of neo-bewilderment, DO NOT turn to Twitter for answers. It's like bobbing for apples in a blood-filled tank of insatiable, starving, speed-freak piranhas with spam on your face. Turn that shit off and eat your phone.

With April now tipping into May, I not only needed to fish local, but I also had to do it with somebody I knew intimately well. It was time to contact Lamont.

Lamont looks like Richard E. Grant, but with the gnarled, belligerent attitude of both Mark E. Smith and Ginger Baker. I've been going fishing with him for almost thirty years; there is nothing we don't know about each other. He and I had just got some exchange tickets for the mid-Ribble beat at New Jumbles Rock, a stunningly picturesque beat under the distant, yet still imposing gaze of Stonyhurst College, an ancient Catholic boarding school in the Jesuit tradition, whatever that means.

The meek can inherit the earth and springboard to a life of purpose, as long as the meeklings can lay their meek hands on £34K per annum, Amen.

Our angling club leases the mid-Ribble from the Stonyhurst

estate. A public footpath known as the Tolkien Trail (the famous author stayed at Stonyhurst several times during the Second World War while visiting his son, who was studying to be a priest) skirts the beat, providing a popular walking route for tourists around what really is a spectacularly beautiful spot, especially on a bright, clear spring day. It is often said with pride (a pride I don't share, by the way) that Tolkien based the Shire region of Middle-earth on the area, and I've often heard walkers say that they are out looking for Hobbits.

The cheeky fuckers!

As I turn into the club car park, I can see that Lamont is already leaning back in the boot of his car with his waders on, ready to go. Dressed in a light short-sleeved shirt, he is reading a self-help book about managing passive aggression, and next to his elbow is another book, entitled Teach Yourself to Meditate, featuring a photograph of a beautiful waterfall on the cover. My heart sings at this physical evidence of his intent to address the deep-seated inner turmoil that so often manifests in erratic, self-destructive behaviour. Lamont isn't one of the worried well, Lamont is something else. I exit my car and start getting changed and setting up, and he greets me with a question.

'How much do you think it is for a bee?'

As always, I am instantly bemused.

'I don't know,' I answer. 'Can you buy them individually?'

'On average, there are thirty thousand in a hive of honeybees,' he says, rubbing his chin. 'This bloke wants forty thousand for his entire hive. I've offered him a penny a bee.'

I could cry with happiness. Man, I've missed this crazy, awkward, abstruse bastard. It's almost overwhelming, the warm sense of glee that consumes me as we walk the well-travelled, ribbon-like path up the beat to where the Ribble meets the river at Calderfoot. He continues on towards a pool named Kelt's Parlour while I start fishing in the run just above Calderfoot, which did have a couple of salmon lies in it before recent flooding changed the geography of the riverbed. Chances are, the lies will have been lost as a result, but you never know for sure until you try.

The sky is a stupidly clear, vivid blue, bordering on turquoise; wide, wired and open, and as I wade the river, I feel relaxed and free. It's left-hand up, which I still find slightly alien, so I double Spey cast when I can. The river height and conditions are as good as it gets, with just under 0.45cm on the New Jumbles Rock gauge; the water is running nearly clear, pulling the fly around in a nice steady fashion. I'm using my 15ft rod and a full floater with an intermediate tip to 15lb maxima, and a very under-dressed, tatty and small self-tied stoat's tail double – a design based on one that I found in a tree – which has caught a few fish elsewhere, despite looking like it's recently exploded. Just before I got in the water, I selected the Neil Young LP After the Gold Rush, and the track Tell Me Why is now gently playing as I cast and step in this lush, green, energised valley of paradise. Behind me, Stonyhurst and Longridge Fell; in front of me, Pendle Hill is bathed in seemingly pewter sunshine. Sand martins complete elegant aerobatics in front of their annual nesting holes, which pockmark the sandbank opposite, and for the next four hours, hope and joy are borne on the breeze as we casually fish our way downstream back to the car.

After rotating each run, fishing slowly through them both, we drop down to a larger spot that we can occupy together, and then stop for some coffee and lunch. With catching a salmon here almost as impossible as teaching a carrot to whistle, we always make sure that lunch is at least a minor triumph. Today, I made an early call to Mark's Bakery and picked up a fresh ciabatta to go with some local Lancashire cheese and ham from Alpe's Butchers, both in Clitheroe. Lamont produces a Golden Delicious and proceeds to slice it up with his disturbingly large Bowie knife, as we both sit with our feet in the river while the long grass cradles us on the bank. I lie back and look up at the big clear sky, only for Lamont to disturb the peace with a sudden outburst.

'Osprey!' he shouts.

Sure enough, here it comes, equal parts majestic and effortless, gliding above our heads as we stare in quiet wonder at its upstream path towards the River Hodder. No words are exchanged until the magnificent bird of prey vanishes from sight, leaving behind two happy old friends wearing the broadest beaming smiles as they revel in the hidden magic of a moment shared.

Eventually, Lamont breaks the idyllic silence.

'Do you think Shaolin monks can drill into their own heads with a hammer drill?' he asks. 'I've seen them do it on YouTube.'

His ability to jolt me out of my own thoughts with a random enquiry is astonishing. We get up and walk to the head of the next run; it's his turn to go through first. As we walk side by side, I give him a smiling tilted glance.

'How long is the drill bit?' I ask.

He goes into the run first, and I give him a fifty-metre head start. As I watch him get started, I imagine Lamont the bee tyrant, losing his patience and getting stung by his frenzied swarm, after making heavy-handed demands that his lazy bees up their honey production.

From a fly-fishing perspective, this run is a pure coffee table book. It's glossy cover quality, the money shot; wide and open, with a broad leaf-wooded far bank, and downstream the copper green domes of Stoneyhurst peeping through the treetops in the distance. The river is shallow gravel on our side, but slowly rises to hip-height roughly a quarter of the way across, where quicker water gives way to a perfect funnel that empties in a flat mirrored glide of around one hundred metres. Double Spey casting here is a pure, unadulterated pleasure; it's possible to cast right down to your backing. Well, not for me, but nearly. Nailing a double Spey always hits all the right notes; all the right notes from your favourite song: the lift, the bend, the turn, the load, the forward release. Just a simple joy in a chaotic world, a split second of perfect. The run finally tumbles over a small weir, which is also the measuring station for New Jumbles Rock. Neither of us have ever hooked a fish here, but we aim to rectify that one day. It just has to happen. I mean, not to blow my own trumpet, but I've had plenty just a hundred metres up on the opposite bank, including a couple over 20lbs (all on the shrimp), and I know those same fish all swam up this run.

Having had our four hours and kept up our one hundred percent record of not hooking a salmon, we start walking back to the car park in mutual agreement that it's going to be an amazing season. This isn't based on any form of scientific evidence; terminal chancers are forever hopelessly hooked on hope. Lamont says he's going home to meditate, do some yoga and carry out some more bee research, but I know that his idea of yoga is furiously chopping wood, while meditation typically amounts to vigorously counting his wood pile. Presumably, his idea of bee research will involve a solitary Google search until he inevitably loses his rag and chucks his steam-powered laptop across his living room.

Namaste.

Ten minutes later, I arrive home a little more energised, relaxed and whole; the sun has been shining on my face and dancing in my soul. The Japanese have a word for it: yugen, a profound sense of universe. My head is nicely filled with yugen, comprising images of herons, sand martins, egrets, kingfishers, common sandpipers, oyster catchers, ospreys, Shaolin monks wielding hammer drills and the highly volatile honeybee market.

The 2021 Ribble salmon season is underway.

A new season is a lovely gift, each trip along the riverbank a glorious tour of natural architecture. Hope springs on every leaf, shoot and blade of grass. All the sounds are tender calls to optimism, a soundscape of purest, honest life and rebirth.

Reggae got soul.

2
King of Clubs

If you really want to hear about it, I may as well give you the full sorry story.

I started lockdown with gleaming intentions to be productive and proactive; to turn that Covid-induced frown upside down and use this forced period of incarceration to my advantage; to produce something brilliant, worthwhile and wholesome. I wanted to emerge into the light with a great new breakout book, something relevant to act as a prism for the times, a reflection of the ever-present, angst-ridden, global, regional and local emergencies that we all now face on a seemingly daily basis. Most of all, though, I wanted to write something popular that could help pay the bills. To malinger this golden opportunity away would be pure folly. That's what an idiot would do, just ignorantly spaff the time away watching and listening to other people's creations.

Such noble thoughts lasted approximately an hour before they were ushered to the back of my mind and firmly shoved down the fire escape, like a drunk being roughly ejected from a nightclub by the local dicky-bowed goon. Those thoughts took serious consideration. Those thoughts took a fastidious work ethic. Those thoughts took guile. Those thoughts took ingenuity. Those thoughts took commitment. Those thoughts took determination and true grit.

'I'm sorry, Mr Gilbraith, but your application to be a better man has been unsuccessful.'

I sat there looking blankly at my laptop for an hour or so, waiting for a thunderbolt of inspiration to stab me sharply between the shoulders before I conceded. Who was I kidding? My three semi-baked horror-show book ideas were just that: half baked. In reality, anything was way more appealing than starting something to reckon and wrestle with for hours a day. Writing and finishing a book would be like trying to tunnel out of Shawshank with a plastic fork and no poster, yet every day I felt pangs of guilt as I flicked on the television and once again binged some overextended ten-part cryptic murder case that had been solved by a YouTuber's cat.

Subscription TV, like being waterboarded with Moet.

Meanwhile, whenever I obediently set off on the one-hour daily family walk or tried to entertain the kids, nagging thoughts about my ongoing procrastination quietly and gently plagued me. Even while playing table tennis on the kitchen table or Play Your sodding Cards Right. Even while playing the vintage game of rebound. Even while playing nearest to the wall with a pound coin. Even while bird watching out of the loft window. Even while painting my house number on to my bins. Even while watching the bloated, liar, clown balloon megalomaniac Boris outside Number Ten. Even while doing all of five minutes of a Joe Wicks workout. No matter how thoroughbred my intentions, I was like a drunk butterfly in a tempest.

However. . .

. . .what I did achieve was to somehow manage to overdose on angling club memberships until I woke up and found I was a fully paid-up member of five angling clubs and associations, with access to roughly thirty miles of the River Ribble and a decent chunk of the (two-hundred-mile round trip) River Eden.

I had joined Prince Albert Angling Society, Ribchester Angling Association, Ribblesdale Angling Association, Carlisle Angling Association and Clitheroe Angling Association Ltd.

Yes, I had gone totally barking-at-the-moon mental.

My 'old normal' club consumption rate was three: Prince Albert, Ribchester and Ribblesdale. Three was just the right number for me to manage, though I still walked the tightrope of choice overload, which can lead to cognitive impairment resulting in your eyes spinning like reels on a fruit machine. The decision to join Carlisle was a heady combination of my two worst qualities: lust and greed. The club had reported a couple of decent years, with featured articles in national mainstream outlets quoting quietly smug anglers catching ten, twenty or even thirty springers on the fly; pulse-raising stuff. One hundred miles suddenly felt like nothing, and it was only one hundred and fifty quid for the whole season. What was the worst that could happen? Truth is, I'd have found a way to join even if I was in a straightjacket; all scepticism, experience, doubt and hesitancy vanished, to be replaced by aggressive overconfidence and a head full of butterflies.

I didn't just want to savour life's juices, I wanted to backstroke in them.

I'm typically a reserved person. I consider things before leaping in, so for me to join five fishing clubs was the equivalent of Led Zeppelin not just trashing their hotel rooms, but also burning down the entire building before snorting the ashes.

Or Kanye West running for president.

The decision to join Clitheroe Angling Association Ltd had been utterly unexpected. It was a small, secretive club with no forwarding address, website or contact details. In short, an enigma, which of course only made me want to be in it even more. In the past, I had occasionally and unsubtly mentioned that I would love to put my name down on their waiting list, only to be shrugged off without so much as an acknowledgement, as it became a running joke for me to hopefully, yet casually, ask those few anglers whom I knew to be members about joining, and for them to artfully change the subject and dodge the question. So, you can imagine my shock and excitement when, during lockdown, I received a clandestine late-night phone call asking if I would be interested in joining for 2021. The offer was underlined in hushed tones by a request to 'keep it under your hat,' and though I was slightly disappointed that the caller had not used one of those voice distortion gadgets you see in horror movies, I knew I couldn't refuse and expect to be asked again.

To get into this club, I would have to pay a one-off fee of £840, plus £420 annual subscription. That's right, £1260, which for me was a truly sphincter-tightening amount, enough to turn my bones to glass, but I couldn't say no and not live to regret it. Price aside, it met my criteria to a T: ridiculously close to home, under fifty members and thirty-two named pools, all of which held perfect fly water. It was a club for life, where, as Lamont wisely put it, you could fish in your slippers, but still I had to be absolutely sure. I could not afford to back the wrong pony. The joining fee was intended to put the prospective candidate in a hideous stress position; they didn't want some half-stepping muppet to come in and then leave the next season. Thus, with £840 putting me firmly in the think tank, I judiciously went and walked the beat from top to bottom.

The lower limit starts at West Bradford bridge (West Bradford population: 778) and is almost continuous double-bank fishing through Grindleton (population: 772) towards Sawley (population: 335). The beat is approximately three miles long, with much of the river sitting within the Ribble Way public footpath route, which is a popular local walk on both banks. I mention the populations of the nearby villages to help paint a picture; this area of Lancashire is not a sprawling metropolis. Clitheroe, with its growing population of seventeen thousand people, is still reassuringly sedate, but compared to West Bradford, Grindleton and Sawley, it is New York City on meth.

I hopped over the stile at West Bradford and began my exploratory wander upstream. The river is still a good size there, with numerous sections worthy of potent admiration. I surveyed it in two halves, bottom and top. Bottom from West Bradford bridge up to Grindleton Bridge, top from Grindleton bridge to the end of the beat at Sawley. I was very familiar with the bottom beat, a favourite walking spot for Sweep, my Bedlington Whippet, where in ten years of regular visits I had never seen a single angler on either bank, ever. Much of this water looked well worth a chuck; premium fly water, especially with a few extra inches on it to help with the carry and flow. All the fishing bird posse were present: biker thug cormorants actively dried off their wings while perched on pronounced rocks; goosanders, dressed in their haute couture plumage, had access to all areas; the ruthlessly efficient grey heron stalked its domain like a clinical terminator unit; two male kingfishers, antagonistically locked in a dramatic aerial turf war, acrobatically tussled and twirled mere inches above the water's surface.

Yep, the gang was all here, and they were glad of the peace and quiet.

My conclusion was that while financially I would rather poke my own eye out with a blunt stick, in real terms this water was nirvana for me.

Huts!

They had their own huts! In a hut, you can daydream and hideout from the world. In a hut, you can shelter from the storm, drink brews, eat, laugh and chat total shite, like making up fictitious aftershave names. Lamont's best effort was Bin Juice by Kevin Clean (advert to be narrated by Lilly Savage). So, once again falling victim to my own desires, I agreed to put my spoon in the soup.

Their club gene pool was about to be substantially watered down.

My epiphany had come on slowly, and only after confusion had subsided to a tolerable level. As an eleven-year-old, my love affair with fishing had bloomed while cutting my teeth on ponds and canals. Then, quite unexpectedly, after years of chasing still-water trout on the fly, I went down the rabbit hole of salmon fishing, where I remained for approximately twenty-seven years. With each turn around the sun, the mood became one of enduring hope sprinkled with an increasingly harsh, gloomy dose of caustic realisation that I could realistically aspire to catch maybe one or two Atlantic salmon in a full season of trying. However, lockdown gave me a chance to reflect and, more importantly, remember; to polish my foggy recollections of the joy of the game, and to harness the energy of the river into my fading spirit. My focus had been too narrow, too formal and too blinkered, but now I planned to fish for everything again, savouring abstract methods and targeting different species; depth-charging nymphs for grayling; long trotting for barbel, dace, roach and chub; dry flying for rising brown trout.

If this post-Covid world was to be the new normal, I was damn sure I was going to fish more frequently, not less; fading away quietly on the river, letting Father Time do his thing, eroding and gently digesting me. Fish more. Write more. Not give a fuck more. That's the bubble I wanted to be in, my own, where I can happily be the sole mayor of Clown Town.

3
Shortbread and Shortcomings

Comfortably numb or pretty vacant, take your pick. My home river, the Ribble, has kicked our teeth in yet again. While I sit in a semi-catatonic state – like Robert De Niro's character in the film Awakenings, slowly swaying on a wooden bench in a surprisingly well-manicured riverside angling club car park – Lamont is electrically charged and highly animated, pacing and preaching his pugilistic linguistics like a twisted, strung-out TV Evangelist, his lithe frame angular and tense (think balletic human praying mantis), his slim face belligerent, caustically sneering and contorted. Our set up, lifeless rods are stood to attention, leaning hopefully against the gate, as Lamont goes on eulogising about our forthcoming April trip to the mighty River Spey.

'Once we get up there,' he decrees, pointing a long finger at me, 'this place will just be a horrible, distant, tit hole, fucked up memory. I may never come back here now. This bastard river is killing us. We need a splash of colour, a dash of hot sauce – a flaming adventure and an urgent intracardiac injection, directly into the heart.' He makes a dramatic, violent stabbing action towards his chest. 'Look at you, for God's sake. Pa-a-athetic! Have you looked in a mirror recently? You look like a doughball shaped into a monument to worry. The light in your eyes is fading, your spark has disappeared. Where even are you?

Everybody can see the cracks. This trip may just save our lives, do you understand? Nod your head if you understand.'

As he finishes off his firing squad monologue, he shines his phone torch at close range across my eyes, checking for signs of life.

He's right, we need a tiny rebellion. There has to be a silver lining; running on empty has a limited shelf-life. The River Spey in April would be a pulse-raising break in the clouds.

After kissing my family goodbye, I skip into Lamont's Northern Soul ambulance to the tune of Sam Dees singing Lonely for You, Baby. If the passenger window was open, I would have torpedoed into the moving vehicle headfirst, a sentiment echoed by Lamont driving out of Clitheroe like a wanted man. He only calms down once we're safely doing ninety miles per hour in the third lane of the M6, on a six-hour drive north that's powered by nothing but pure optimism.

The conversation starts with the potential whereabouts of our dead friend's sacred notebook (Ahab's Book of Lies), which lists every spot where he had ever caught a salmon on the Ribble over a fifty-year period. We've recently been sent a cryptic map and letter from the grave, delivered by Ahab's brother, the secretive and elusive Quint. Ahab had apparently buried his journal, but he left Lamont and I a series of vague clues as to its location somewhere along the banks of the Ribble. This inspires roughly one hundred miles of speculation that eventually gives way to a teeth-grinding River Spey stat bomb powerful enough to leave a path of information overload in its wake: optimum water temperature, height, wind direction and air pressure, plus detailed performance reviews of the all the middle river beats. Apparently, our beat has been punching above its weight this season, having already recorded thirty-three fish.

If only all our fishing was done virtually on the internet, we could swap our waders for white lab coats. Science says it will be easy; over five thousand salmon and grilse caught on the River Spey in 2020. Science says that's four thousand five hundred and fifty more than our home river.

The Ribble vs the Spey, like me trying to drop Tyson Fury; it's not a fair fight. We even have faith that Terrence (according to Lamont, Terrence Cracking is a woodland spirit who helps salmon anglers) will help us on our quest, especially after Lamont conducts a short prayer to him while having a piss at the services, meaning that with both science and religion on our side, our luck requirements are well and truly boxed off. Not to mention, on my Spey debut in 2019, I hooked and landed a salmon on only my second cast, so my confidence is soaring with each turn of the tyres.

In Terrence we trust.

The last twenty miles seem like a back-road sixty; as the distance between us and our destination reduces, so does our patience. The only consolation is that it's Sunday, and since we're not allowed to fish the river until tomorrow, rushing serves no real purpose.

A few pints and an early night, like a kid on Christmas Eve.

Upon arrival at our digs in Archestown, Lamont quickly installs himself as captain for the week, thus claiming the perk of a double bed and private en-suite bathroom. The title also makes him responsible for deciding the rota for pools we'll be fishing. Our rented beat, Kinermony, takes three rods. There are six of us, which means half a rod each. Confused? You will be. Splitting rods makes the trip more affordable as we pair up to share the cost, each fishing an hour on and an hour off. Our beat is split into two; the top half comprises three pools to fish through: Little Turn, Rind and Dykie; the bottom is one long pool, easily big enough to take two rods at once, known as the Boat Pool.

Lamont Fun Fact: when employed as a hospital theatre porter, he once knocked himself out with ether while an operation was taking place in the next room. He woke up on the floor and, still swaying, returned to the theatre to continue his duties. The surgeon informed an anaesthetised Lamont that he would be ready for the next patient in an hour, so could he please go and ensure that he was clean-shaven from nipple to knee. Lamont then arrived at the patient's room and hopefully offered him the option of shaving himself, only for the patient, who could have been mistaken for a gorilla, to remove his gown and place his hands behind his head, before cheerfully replying, 'No, that's OK. I think I'll leave it to the expert.'

I am sharing a rod with my friend Karl, AKA the Heron. He and I fish fairly regularly on our club waters in Clitheroe. If he had his own Top Trumps card, he would score a perfect ten for effort. His demented internal dialogue, describing exactly where the salmon are, is on a permanent loop, and he has a work ethic that makes a hummingbird look lazy. He is currently positioned in a heavy current in the head of the Little Turn; we've seen maybe twenty sparkling fresh, fit fish since we arrived at the top beat. Davey, our ghillie, has confirmed that these are all running fish, and I reckon there are more of them here right now than I've seen in the last two years on the Ribble.

Oh, baby!

Davey recommends a skinny, sparsely-dressed Wille Gunn tube on a slow-sink tip to a full floater. The Heron has put a faster sink tip on, but has gone along with a threadbare Willie Gunn, and I am sat on a bench overseeing him while he makes his double Spey. He makes his cast and a fish enters the pool; we both watch keenly as his cast swings around, covering the target. Anticipation is on high alert; Karl watches his cast linger on the dangle before starting the almost Tai Chi-like motion of sending it out again. Everything is in motion, like a reed bending in the wind; the water, the rod, the fish, the fly and the angler, nothing is static. Step and cast, lift, draw, sweep, turn and shoot. A cosmos within the cosmos. Beauty briefly becoming infinite.

After an hour, it's my turn to spin the wheel. I wade into the fearsome Rind, a brutish bastard full of boulders and very quick, fast-pressing, forceful water. I go in up to my waist and set my feet; I am using my twelve-year-old, fifteen-foot, three-piece Hardy Demon. Call me old fashioned but I'm still hanging-on in there with carbon fibre, sure I've seen chop-sticks but I've already got a fork. I love this rod; through frequent use and many adventures, it holds a piece of me inside its fibres; the smooth cork handle has ingested my very DNA. We are getting old together, I know every contour, every mark and every scratch. Sounds ridiculous, doesn't it? Having affection for an inanimate object (I Googled it, so you don't have to – good grief!), AKA objectophilia or anthropomorphism, or just daft old git.

I'm OK with any of those labels.

Using a Mackenzie Spey line, I can almost cast to the backing. I feel the rod load and cast square; the fish count has climbed to forty-odd, the whole scene is glowing with spring-powered luminosity. Davey and his three labradors are all seated on the manicured bank behind me, daffodils are in bloom and Karl has made a brew and a roll-up. He's ambling back to stroke the dogs.

'Your line's coming around lovely,' he shouts, smiling. 'Any second now, mate.'

For fifty-nine minutes, I carefully cast and step. Each attempt could be the one; it's a mini opera of hope, desire and disappointment. I change to a one-inch copper Wille Gunn tube on a five-foot fast-sink tip; fish show and pass me on every cast. Come the fifty-eighth minute, doubt quietly starts its nagging song.

Maybe this is how my week will play out, I think fleetingly, before quickly nailing that awful thought back in its box. Nah, no fucking way can we blank.

One hour in, and I'm already on the verge of writing off the whole week.

At lunch, all six of us compare similar stories: an abundance of spring salmon seen, but nothing pulling. The height is a hot topic, with four people, including Davey, disagreeing about the current level. Apparently, all gauges are not the same.

'You need to subtract eight inches from that,' Davey says, with a wry smile.

I'm running out of fingers and toes while dissecting the complex rules of reading a gauge until, eventually, after further lively debate, we learn that the current height is one foot and eight inches (i.e., perfect). In terms of tactics, we seemingly have it covered with a spread bet of sink rates, sizes, dressings and fly styles, each angler trying a slight variation on the other in the hope of picking the lock and solving the puzzle. The lunch time consensus is that it's only a matter of time before one of us gets lucky and hooks up.

As we're getting up to leave, Lamont says within everybody's earshot, 'Failure is the pillar of success.'

After a very enjoyable lunch and unwelcome interlude – having to pause while fish were showing seems so wrong – Karl and I drop down to the Boat Pool, where we immediately see large splashes and other signs of movement. I decide to put on a substantial copper half-inch tube with a blue hackle and long black wing, as fishing the same fly over and over on some lobotomised infinity loop was driving me crazy. It's nice to have at least the illusion of some involvement in the process, this isn't click and collect. The intention is to let it swing at around two-feet deep, hopefully annoying as many passing fish as possible. At the head of the pool, I can comfortably get within a few feet of the far bank, with my unmended square cast coming around like a flying C would. First cast, and a bright-silver double-figure fish leaps my main line, before a running fish head-and-tails ten feet downstream from my fly.

These fish aren't hanging about!

Every cast a chance, I remind myself with each step and repeat. Every cast a chance.

The same multicoloured hope loop of internal monologue begins with every chuck, my mind exploding like a Jackson Pollock abstract. Fish all over: nothing. Fish all over: nothing. Halfway down the pool, I change to a size-ten double Willie Gunn, the fly I had success with in the very same spot three years ago.

Nothing.

My hour up, I trudge out of the river with my faithful, reliable waders bilaterally weeping internal Spey tears just above both knees (honestly, I may as well start fishing in shorts and rubber surf socks. Suck it up, buttercup!). Karl gets the thumbs up to start his hour-long shift at the top of the run, and I can see the excitement glimmering in his eyes as fish are well and truly all over the place.

In the strikingly brutalist, utilitarian green tin hut, I put the kettle on and examine the local job market on my phone. A local shortbread factory is looking for a groundsman; this glamorous position comes with its own cottage and a car. As an added incentive, if you live in Aberlour you can join the association water of Aberlour Anglers for – wait for it – £120 a year.

Grab yourself a chair and sit down while you think about all the wondrous possibilities.

Looking through my fly box, I play with the thought of what a really sparse Willie Gun could be called. Maybe just a Gunn or a Willie, I muse. For every strand of hair stripped from the pattern, lose a letter until you only have a G or a W left.

Before I know it, the Mummy returns; Karl is at the end of his hour. I watch him walk up the bank dragging his right leg as he announces, 'My bastarding stocking foot's full of bastard water.'

Waders. All are shite, Amen.

The group has arranged to meet at the Aberlour Hotel at seven o'clock for an evening meal, giving us all a chance to regroup, shower and change. Nothing has been caught, and that's with two of our party being proper veterans. Robbie and Richard have been having a week up here since 1968, and, both now in their mid-seventies, they still fish hard and can tell a tale or two. Ideal companions; our warm urgency blends with their cold front of patience and acceptance. Don't panic is their ethos, just enjoy the process. Richard reminds me of Ahab. He is quiet and methodical, with a sharply-focussed sense of purpose. Robbie is full of questions about beats you've fished, fish you've caught and clubs you've been in. He also seems worryingly obsessed with the height gauge, to the point where I think he could be a glimpse of an older, wiser version of Lamont.

Hey, you never know. Think positive, etc.

Over chicken linguine and a pint, we discuss the job specifics of the groundskeeper role at the shortbread factory. I pose the question of how many tons of shortbread a day the factory produces, inciting a debate that lasts a while and provides a decent distraction from another round of tired salmon fishing theory chat. Karl reckons fifty tons a day. Lamont dismisses this estimate out of hand.

'The roads would be gridlocked with sugar lorries,' he scoffs. 'Fifty tons? Not a chance!'

It's decided that Lamont will phone the factory in the morning to apply for the groundskeeper job, after which he'll fill in the blanks regarding shortbread production.

During breakfast the next morning, I can't help noticing Karl's expression as he samples his morning brew. His face is fizzing like salt on a slug, forming a mask of complete displeasure.

'This Scottish sugar is miles sweeter than ours,' he laments, noticing my noticing. This automatically raises my left eyebrow before he adds, 'It's at least eight times sweeter.'

Both eyebrows now raised, I'm still processing the notion of 'Scottish sugar' when Lamont begins inspecting the jar. He sticks his long, 'ET phone home' of an index finger into the sugar and has a taste. A look of total scorn then crosses his face as he exclaims, 'Operation numb nuts, it's caster sugar. Scottish sugar! You need locking up.'

My eyebrows have found their way around the back of my head, as Karl rightly appears crestfallen.

What chance do the salmon have?

From the small car park on the top beat, Lamont makes the call to the shortbread factory. Even Davey the ghillie is listening intently.

'Hello, yes. I'm enquiring about the groundskeeper's job. . .Yes please, put me through.'

A few tense moments pass before he's connected to the relevant department.

'Hi, yes. I'm a former greens keeper,' he tells them. 'I worked at Royal Lytham – that course took some clinical management. Faldo loved me. It wasn't just raking bunkers and fiendish pin positions, believe me. What I'd like to know is the state of your equipment. Is the mower a sit-on or push along? . . . Ride-on, that's good. It shows a real commitment to quality.' He nods his head while giving us the thumbs up as the person at the other end continues to sell the job. 'That all sounds perfect. How much shortbread do you make in a day, by the way? . . .Really? Oh, that's very interesting. Wow! Now, I have one more question for you. When I'm at work, will I be expected to work all the time or are there some areas on the grounds that are good hiding places? . . . Oh, that's a shame. I'm a great believer in the importance of a post-lunch nap – good for productivity. A nap promotes productivity like yoga fights gravity. I'm incredibly agile. Anyway, thanks for the info. I will let you know my decision in due course. Bye now.'

That's entertainment!

'Ten tons a day,' Lamont says laughingly. 'Twenty when they do shortbread fingers. There's an international audience for those, you see.'

With one mystery now solved, all that remains for us to crack is the height gauge and the salmon. Both seem impenetrable.

The beat rotation is still in force as all six of us toil for the next couple of days, during which time the fish sightings have halved and the sun has been shining. It all feels a bit hopeless, like poor old Charlie Brown trying to kick the football. I wonder if maybe it's due to us fishing the same pools repeatedly. When I'm in the water, I still have a feeling of hope and confidence, but something feels off. The rules have me constricted; on my home waters, I can mooch from club beat to club beat at will 24/7. I know I've already mentioned the Ribble's near total absence of salmon, but at least I'm free to fecklessly roam about there, instead of being restrained like Harry Houdini trapped in a straightjacket, fighting for freedom in a submerged sack.

My focus and aim have subconsciously shifted over time. Standing in the winning pool until my line goes tight is obviously not the draw it once was, but if all that turned me on was catching, I could go to any number of commercial trout fisheries and nab jumbo rainbows. Those small lakes are like crazy golf is to real golf; like French cricket to a test match or bounce-backs to eleven-a-side on a full pitch. Quick and fun, yes, but nowhere near as fulfilling. Contentment comes in many forms and colours; it's not the catching that juices me up, it's the fishing and the hope of catching. Fishing never lets me down. The feeling of being involved in the whole process is compelling, hence four hours of wandering and wondering on the Ribble being my idea of heaven. It's nice to have a change and exciting to see fish, but this week away thing is not my bag. I like home too much; I appreciate what I already have. I miss my wife and kids, I miss the dog and I miss the Ribble. I miss being free to explore.

From catatonic state to homesick soft lump.

What's it called when you fall in love with your captors? Stockholm syndrome? Whatever it is, I've got it bad, and that ain't good!

By Wednesday evening, I've decided to leave at Friday lunch, a day early. Meanwhile, Lamont has hooked up with a double-figure salmon in the Boat Pool, having cleverly orchestrated a rare take by using a full floater with only a three-foot leader (no tip) and a hitched sunray shadow. The fish snatched at it just as it came on the dangle; the scrap lasted five minutes until the hook finally pulled. Lamont let out a subatomic scream of, 'FUCK YOU, TERRANCE!' leaving anglers on the opposite bank looking equal parts alarmed and beautifully bewildered. I just hope one of them was called Terry.

No other fish are hooked this week. All the stars seem broken.

I fish the last two days trying everything except tying on a Chicken linguine, even though my double Spey is now so on-point, I could easily cast a plateful. On Thursday evening, we have a marvellous bankside barbecue of prime local steak and boiled spuds – best steak I've ever had – before asking ourselves why we didn't do this every evening.

Idiots.

Science is the winner, too. On Wednesday, Karl took a tumble in the Rind on his way out of the river, soaking him through. That evening, he was overly keen to dry out his wading jacket, so I suggested hanging it up in the shower and allowing it to drip dry overnight. Instead, he found the tumble dryer, and with some of his audience giddy and happily tipsy on various single malts and a pleasant stream of space cakes, it was only a thirty-minute wait before we had the results of this experiment.

His jacket now looks like a half-mast matador's traje de luces.

That's entertainment!

With Lamont agreeing to get a lift home with Karl on Saturday afternoon, I can make an early exit in his car on Friday morning. I've had enough.

Apparently, Lamont went to the river at 6am to fish the Boat Pool, whereas I'm taking the scenic route through Aberlour, past the shortbread factory. As I sit at the traffic lights, a particularly smart-looking red and yellow sit-on mower pulls up slowly alongside me; at the wheel sits a grinning and very smug-looking Lamont, resplendent in a yellow hi-vis vest and matching hard hat. Through my now lowered passenger window, he gleefully shouts, 'I'm on probation for two weeks,' before gliding left through the factory gates.

Headed to a bright new future? Not quite. Three days into his probationary period, he is found soundly asleep in a shed next to his sit-on mower. He tries to argue his case by claiming he was in actual fact meditating as a means of increasing his personal productivity, but it's no use. Security quietly and discretely escorts him off site, and he gracefully migrates back to the comforting bosom of his Lancashire-based open care facility, the Ribble Valley.

4
Body Count

How times change. Recently, I have been lamenting our past. Reflection is a gift often opened during lean times; I've opened it along with a dusty stack of vintage salmon books and game fishing magazines. Without exception, the monochrome narrative is the same: how many and how big? That's the accompanying chorus to every photograph, a song sung to the tune of the green-eyed glint of lust, complementing images of the author proudly displaying dead fish in clinically choreographed ascending order. Success was a body count, measured using the cold, emotionless rod of bottom-line economics. A narrative never questioned, driven by the pushers and peddlers who are after your cash.

Killer tackle, killer price and a killer beat.

Beaming smiles abound while glassy eyes gaze out euphorically, conveying the message that I, too, could be like them. Chase the trophy more efficiently, more effectively; more sport, more fun; more greed, and like Gordon Gekko unashamedly quipped in the movie Wall Street, 'Greed is good.' Well, the real-life Gekko types rode that money train until it derailed in 2007, before getting bailed out by good old Joe Public, no questions asked. Nobody went to jail, they all just boarded an even faster train and started popping the corks on new bottles of fizz. They got more and we got less, again;

furrowed brows all round as we throw up our arms and cry foul. We often hear the wrinkled argument that there would be a brain drain if we cut financial services bonuses. Good. Put them all on a remote desert island together, with all their big brains, and see how long they last trading financial services between themselves. Whatever the case, our narrative in all the big glossy magazines remains the same.

How many? How big?

Hindsight can be used in a witheringly pious manner. Truth be told, I was just as bad. If blanking on a paid fishery, we all had a rule-pushing, go-to method of ensuring that an empty haul would be avoided. Thus, I claimed the annual limit of two salmon right up until the last one I killed in 2012. Who drove this narrative? Every book, catalogue and magazine that revelled in the business of results, the bottom line. What did you catch? How big? How many? Captions foamed at the mouth in exclaiming: The fish is killed, unhooked and admired! Don't get me wrong, the narrative looked over its shoulder in those publications back then, too. There would be questions like, 'Are we catching as many as we used to?' but the hollow-tipped issue of sustainability was never addressed. That word seemingly hadn't even been invented yet; file under 'do-gooder.' It was a word to be avoided like a bad smell, lest it raise questions that were bad for business.

Personally, I have seen this trend of 'win everything' very slowly change over my forty-three years of angling. The emphasis on method and quality of the encounter, coupled with a desire for a more holistic experience, is winning out. Of course, Big Media was the slowest to change; in thrall to advertisers and shareholders, their entire model was based on owning every title, sucking up content for bigger profits. Bigger circulation meant larger ad revenue; think of the kids' game

Hungry Hippos and you've got the picture. They wanted your time for free; you should be honoured to be featured.

'What, you want paying as well!?'

Their MO was owning your content, giving them complete, irrevocable control of the narrative. 'Sell! Sell! Sell!' might as well have been 'Kill! Kill! Kill!'

The final winners were the multinational media conglomerates. The losers? Turn on the news. Bottom-line accountancy has blindly made corporations powerful enough to change laws in their favour, to lobby for whatever they want, and what they want is always more. Freedom of choice is a thin veil in Big Media. How do you want yours regurgitated? Three companies own 90% of the UK print media market – three! Six companies own 90% of the entire mass media and distribution market in the US.

Joseph Heller and Kurt Vonnegut were once at a party on Shelter Island, hosted by a billionaire hedge fund manager. Vonnegut said to Heller, 'Do you know this guy made more money in one day than your entire sales of Catch-22?' Heller responded, 'Yes, but I have something he will never have: ENOUGH.'

Incredibly, money can seemingly wash away sins. The Catholic Church sold indulgences for cash, so if you wanted to diminish your sin count, you could just send a little cash their way. Send enough, and they would make you a saint – fact. Cash for privileges, cash for knighthoods, cash for sports-washing (FIFA World Cup in Qatar, anybody?). Want your horrible product green-washed? Saddle up a lovable celebrity and show them the money. Want your reputation cleansed? Well, there could be a public relations company that would be able to spin things in your favour, but it's going to cost you. The long answer and the short answer always seem to be the same: send cash.

'The price of everything and the value of nothing,' as Oscar Wilde famously put it.

How big? How many?

I have written this after another trout session with my friend Lamont. We sat in the hut and watched a sudden spring shower while eating homemade sandwiches and drinking coffee from a Thermos flask. Brief rain interlude aside, the weather was mild and warm in a classic spring evening sense, and we just talked. Man, did it feel good.

You could almost feel the hut exhale as the shower drifted through the valley and we drifted back to the riverbank, where I asked Lamont what he thought his definition of being complicit was.

'I only applied for a job building and fitting a monorail,' he began with a smile. 'The interview was light enough. The doctor with the cat on his lap was pleasant, all milk and cookies. He said it was a long-term project that involved sleeping on-site, before asking if I would be missed. Now, I did think that was kind of odd, and then he asked if I had ever been in the armed forces. When I told him no, he seemed a little put out. The site itself was interesting, though. The monorail was to link up a base on an island to run underground into an extinct volcano. I don't think this doctor was your average GP.

'Complicity,' he went on. 'At what point does the monorail worker think, "Hang on a minute?" There's a load of complicit people in situations they never envisaged. Start as a monorail engineer, end up as an armed guard in a maniac's private army. Coercion with a smile. The monorail guy thought he was on a good number, a nice tickle. He never gave it a second thought until the missiles glided by him on the monorail he had helped to build.'

He is expressively pleased with himself.

Leaning with my back against a very large and old conker tree, I laugh as he looks at me with a hint of devilment in his eyes. It's time to head back; the river must be crossed. While scrambling up the bank out of the water, I ask for clarification.

'So, you're either assembling the megalomaniac's monorail or you're dismantling it? It's as binary as that?'

'Exactly,' he calls back over his shoulder, having gone ahead of me to gingerly jump the wobbly, creaking stile.

Back at the car, we say our goodbyes and I am left to pursue further private reflection on the drive home. It went something like this:

I'm a wizened, tired fifty-four-year-old, who is so jaded by all the daily rampant, effluent discharge of the vulgarly affluent that I'm starting to involuntarily mutter, twitch and develop a stoop while walking. The crow's feet under my eyes are wearing snowshoes because the scales are so clearly tipped in the top five percent's favour on repeat again and again, smiling as they're fucking us all front and back in broad daylight. Governed by greed, not need; polluted rivers and private water profits, with a side order of obscene bonuses; tax breaks for the wealthy and food banks becoming normal, as communities are sucked dry by vampire corporations and mutilated by faceless multinationals.

Just for the record, I am not an economist, but here goes. Let's take the example of a health care professional. The National Health Service is the nation's largest employer, so let's say we pay a nurse a starting salary of £30k a year. That nurse pays tax on the £30k, meaning it goes straight back into 'our' system. Nurses don't bank offshore or use a tax avoidance scheme, and they pay their national insurance contributions. The rest of their wage is spent in their communities; the money doesn't just vanish into some multinational bank account. Clearly, this results in money being distributed within a community, which in turn prospers, so does it not make sense to pay them enough to incentivise others to view nursing as a viable career path, rather than simply grinding them to dust and spitting them out? Invest in the system, don't strangle it. Money in the shared hands of the many, rather than the grasping fists of the few. There are one hundred and seventy-seven billionaires in the UK. One million seconds equals eleven days. One billion seconds equals thirty-one years.

Chew on that.

How much did one of the energy giants make in one quarter again, six billion? Six billion in profit!

Sedate me. Get out the rum, open the wine and get a bake on. Reality is too monstrous. When will they ever just have ENOUGH?

Once in a while, I just need to bark at the moon, so please forgive me this self-indulgence. I do, however, still see the odd glimpse of shining light breaking through the clouds in the distance. Shop local, shop independent; live purposely within your community; invest in something that sees the bigger picture in high definition, a small, valuable, delicate flickering flame in the wind, trying not to get extinguished; something that can help slowly change culture, not because it wants a golden-diamond ten square miles of prime real estate, but because it believes in what it's doing and who it's doing it for. That's why I love the two independent magazines I occasionally write for, Fly Culture and Fallons Angler. It takes some balls to break the wheel of big media. Thankfully, more people seem to be thinking the same way.

I think we are all just so very tired of all the constant bile. So, if you find yourself inside a metaphorical volcano casually tightening a nut on a megalomaniac's monorail, think on.

On a brighter note, late-May has broken the vein and injected four months of summer. I don't rush summer: dog walks, hill climbs, picnics and fishing club work parties; hunting for Ahab's Book of Lies. Fishing activity slows as the river drops; it's mostly just the occasional shot in the dark for a sea trout or some lazy day of dry fly-fishing for brown trout. With low water comes additional problems: water temperature, flow and algae.

Happily, the more extreme weather is absent, for now at least, allowing the river to breathe easy.

5
Flies (Zeros to Heroes)

Lamont and I are taking a well-trodden desire line across a field, him out in front, leading the way with his usual brisk pace. We are excited, with a palpable sense of febrile urgency; we think we know where there is a six-pound brown trout. Lamont is at his pulpit, preaching venomously, while I follow along feeling acutely happy, almost to the point of giddiness.

'A rare blossom and sublime art form is fly dressing,' his left hand caresses the air as he speaks. 'Patience, skill and imagination are the fly dresser's tools. Each stroke bespoke, each action both question and answer. The long winter nights are when they ply their silent trade, illuminated by the log burner's warm glow, so at least you know where the really weird fuckers are, kept busy and off the streets. Imagine the crime statistics if it wasn't for fly tying?'

'You reckon history would be different if we occupied certain people with the right obsessions?' I ask, cheerfully warming to the theme.

'Absolutely,' he confirms. 'Putin might be selling flies on eBay instead of feeling the need to invade Ukraine. Nobody ever invaded a country to get a jungle cock cape, and if the greased piglet, liar king Boris was glued to his vice, working on the nuances of a selection of intricate and dainty dry flies – imagine! No bullshit bus. No parties. No kipping at the climate summit.

No hiding in a fridge. No having a belligerent, dishonest man-child as leader of the country.'

I immediately start compiling a mental list of other politicians, entertainers and celebrities whom I wish had vanished down the rabbit hole of the fly vice and into blissful obscurity. Leading the way is Victorian super snake, enemy of the poor and professional tax dodger Jacob Rees-Smug, as I picture what life would be like if an all-consuming interest had kept him in his box and off the mean streets of Mayfair.

Spirited conversation has spurred us along a march to the top of our Nappa beat on the Ribble, which is premium trout water. Both banks are gripped by mangled, lurching trees, dense bushes and a general tangle of limbs, roots and unchecked undergrowth; it's like being in the moshpit at a Rage Against the Machine gig. The pools are full of deep holes and boulders; it's the kingdom and realm of truly epic trout. We both find it extremely challenging to fish, but the risk-to-reward ratio is high if you're lucky enough to get it right and keep your game tight, so let's let the funk flow.

Lamont lowers himself down gingerly into the water at the head of the pool. Sitting in the grass, I get my notebook out and jot down some thoughts on fly dressing.

Everybody has an opinion. I've seen the most gloomy, dog-eared, twisted and gnarled flies catch fish; anglers lovingly grooming some tatty, charred, hungover remains of a traumatised Ben Gunn castaway that's narrowly survived some extreme heavy lifting and ugly savagery, desperately trying to blow, stroke and resuscitate it back into shape, so it can mimic that sublime magic trick.

Under-dressed, overdressed; too big, too small; too heavy, too light; too long, too short. Wrong materials, old patterns, new patterns; hitched, unhitched; Rapala knot, lucky and unlucky;

slow movement, fast movement; and all these simultaneous observations every time you open your fly box, your poor head's processing speed like the wheel of death buffering your livestream. If you're like me, picking out a winner can lean towards the side of perplexing. I catch so few salmon that experimentation is a high-risk occupation, so I tend to go for flies that have done the business in the past. The old fish with an element of confidence ploy. Evolution is a slow process on the banks of this river. In fact, it may have thrown itself off a cliff.

The sheer amount of salmon fly patterns should give any reasonable human a clue as to what a crapshoot it is. There are enough variants and variations to fill books so thick, you could use them to stand on while changing a light bulb. Pot-bellied Pig, Red Francis, Cascade, Atomic Cascade, Turbo Stoat's Tail, Pig Francis, Cascading Pig. . .who knows? Not me. Right place? Right time? Maybe. . .

Most of us rotate the squad, like Pep Guardiola on a cold, wet night at Burnley. Wise old Pep and his many cool jumpers, he knows he can put the under-seventeens on and still walk it by at least five. I guess success comes down to the gene pool you're fishing in. Most of our big guns get a run-out during a session. The squad is punctuated by some new signing, a real hot shot who has rewritten the record books on the continent, recommended by the scouts on a distant forum – or who caught your drunken glad eye on eBay. Another must-have sure thing that will muster a fish like a magician with a wizard's sleeve.

These fancy new signings don't have long to make an impact, though. Not when Alan Shearer is in your fly box, and he's almost back to full fitness and wants his place back. With each empty cast, you're reminded of Shearer's many glory days, as the temptation to hook the new lad and bring on the tried and tested goal machine becomes increasingly hard to suppress.

My Alan Shearer is a street-fighting stoat's tail, which looks like it's been chewed up by an escalator and then cut out by the local fire brigade, before eventually being rehabilitated in Charlie Manson's basement. It's a nervous wreck of a fly, a shadow of its former self; size-twelve hook, tatty black hackle, silver wrapping now flapping with a hint of a clipped yellow stump. I think I might have found it hung up in a tree somewhere. Those types of found flies are my favourites, lost by an unlucky angler and found by a lucky one, or so I would like to believe. I start and finish every session with it, mostly using it on the dropper with a lightly-dressed Willie Gunn on point. Are they better than anything else in the box? Who knows? Certainly not me. All I know is that when you do manage to perform the miracle magic trick and actually hook an Atlantic salmon, the fly that cracks the code is one that stays in the memory every time the box is opened. Just like when you bought a vinyl record, it makes an indelible mark on the mind; you retain the when, why and where, feeling a warmth that's absent with a clinical online stream or download.

Lamont raises a hand in the air, snapping me out of my salmon fly reverie. When I worked at the cracker factory, one of my jobs was to communicate using British Sign Language with hearing-impaired students, so I'm pretty good at non-verbal communication. I note that Lamont's outstretched finger is pointing upstream to a large boulder and a lone overhanging branch near the far bank, indicating that a nice fish has just moved. It's a tricky cast, requiring him to slowly wind in to check his leader and change his tippet. He then adds three feet of Stroft GTM mono and puts on a plump-looking March Brown; the first cast he makes is short of the target, and we both watch as the fly dead-drifts harmlessly past. Next cast is longer and right on the money; the fly vanishes and Lamont lifts into the fish, taking a second to allow himself a grin over his shoulder. The game is afoot, and after a feisty romp around the pool, our contestant gently unhooks and returns a fish of around two pounds.

It pains me to say it, but this was a measured, accomplished piece of angling. The room for error was vast; the tangle of jungle behind him on the raised bank and the grasping overhead branches could have easily affected the outcome. It begs the question, would an Accrington brick, common or garden, screw-top angler such as I make that cast in only two attempts? Maybe, baby, but I doubt it. In my case, it'd be less a cast, more a blinkered lucky dip, like giving the eight ball a decent crack around a pool table in the hope it drops in a pocket.

Lamont's peacock tail is up in full vibrant feather display, his chest puffed out as he struts to the next pool down. Bracing myself for a forceful stream of his verbal sewage, I quietly drop into the water while he sits in the grass, his gears visibly turning as he clears his throat.

Today's weapon of choice is a newly acquired second-hand, ten-foot Vision Mag four-weight, with a vintage Orvis Battenkill reel holding a mystery dry line. The second-hand tackle is a recent purchase, part of a job lot of fly gear that I planned on splitting up and parting out, so I'm reasonably confident that the line matches the rod. Copying Lamont, I too have put on a March Brown, but I've also put a drop of Gink on the back, making it sit slightly higher in the water. This spot has been kind to me in the past; I've caught five salmon on the fly from this pool.

Let me just quantify that last stat. It's five in twelve years of fishing it, and two of those fish came in consecutive casts. Those numbers are grim reading, like a winter electricity bill, but the sound of the river has the sort of fragrant tone that lifts the spirit and engenders belief. The water envelops me up to my thighs, pressing against my body. Seeing movement everywhere, my mind is both focussed and empty at the same time.

'Don't stick it in the tree, you dozy bastard,' a prone Lamont calls out through a mouthful of a Roy Porter's chicken, leak and ham pie.

Jolted from a state of Keats-like hypnosis, I take a moment to reset myself. There is a narrow window to cast upstream and let the fly drift under the overhanging, grasping clamour of branches on the far bank; my cast comes to rest in the perfect spot, fully engaged, stooped and primed for a take. The river carries the fly down under the branches, where it's at its most vulnerable, like a lost drunk tourist outside Amsterdam Central railway station after midnight, a heavy scene for the unwary and undertrained. It makes this first pass unscathed, and then same again second and third casts, looking every bit the happy wanderer until attempt four sees it drift down a slim corridor of uncertainty where, suddenly and quietly, a large swirl confirms its disappearance.

Lifting the rod, I know instantly that this is big. Sea trout? I dare to wonder. Salmon? A huge brown trout?

'Don't blow it, el cabron,' Lamont crows happily, now sitting bolt upright.

The fish charges and slaps me about for a bit; sometimes, you just get a vibe that it's not going to come off, but then the fireworks subside and I net an absolute corker of a brownie, at least twice the size of Lamont's. The fish is unhooked, and I clumsily photograph the back of its head while it enters a brief state of recovery. Its colours are worthy of admiration, and I make a mental note to paint some trout-spot-inspired abstracts at the nearest opportunity. At a guess, I'd make it maybe five or six pounds, but I don't really care. The last brownie I caught that was anywhere near as big would have been on Loch Mask, way back in the eighties.

A home river gives its love slowly; it's no place for a one-night stand. This relationship is a long-term trip, a journey of highs and lows, requiring understanding, compromise and trust. Love absorbed through every pore, its roots run deep and its flowers bloom until its energy is yours.

Smug Porter's pork pie time for me. We sit chatting for a good thirty minutes before fishing the rest of the top half of the beat and Lamont lands another three feisty brownies, all between the one and one-a-half pound mark. During our casual chat, he tells me about a time he shot at a robin with an air pistol when he was twelve. I'll faithfully repeat his version of how it went down, but do bear in mind that he's had over forty years in the editing suite by this point, so I'm guessing he'll have sanded the edges while playing through every frame.

'I was a keen bird-watcher,' he begins. 'Witton Park in Blackburn had a bird-watching club. We would walk through all the woods and tick off all the birds we had seen. The head warden was called Bob – he must have been in his late thirties. Outdoors type, always in green clothing, with a bald, tanned head like a baked bean. He left us to it. The club would meet on a Saturday morning at the visitor centre, which was a collection of stone barns and cottages in the middle of the park. Bob would greet us and then send us on our way.

'At school, I had borrowed a Webley Tempest .22 air pistol from a boy in my class. It was stashed in the poacher's pocket of my wax jacket, and as soon as we got away from the visitor centre the pistol, it was out. First, I shot a few trees. Too easy. Then, about fifteen feet away, a robin landed on the rim of a nearby litter bin. Thinking I was Dirty Harry, I took aim and fired. At that exact same moment, Bob appeared. The robin flew off, and Bob had some sort of mental episode and went completely bat shit, snatching the gun and escorting me to his office inside the visitor centre, where he phoned both the cops and my parents. Naturally, I was terrified, realising that I was in the deepest shit of my young life. A caution was given by the local bobby, and, flanked by my parents, I offered the defence that I hadn't known what I was doing was wrong. Still glowing crimson, Bob looked right into me and said calmly, "Ignorance of the law is no excuse," while tearing up my little yellow bird-watchers club card as he spoke.

'On the way home, I asked my dad if ignorance of the law was an excuse. "Depends who you are, son," he answered. "But in your case, it isn't. No playing out for two weeks."

He was visibly crestfallen in recalling this tale, becoming increasingly animated as the seemingly still very vivid memories came flooding back.

'For every action, there's a reaction,' he shouts, pointing a finger in my direction. 'The only good thing about the whole shitty incident was that I had missed the poor robin.'

As is often the case with Lamont's stories, wrapped in there like a terrified hostage is a moral. You can draw your own conclusions about what that moral may be; don't ask me for answers, I'm just an observer before the lights go out one final time. He tells me he had also been thrown out of the Cubs, aged nine, for foul language. He had sewn on to his jumper some sort of technical knot-tying badge that hadn't been earned, an act that the Akela viewed as a most heinous rule violation, worthy of a dose of punishment in the form of a size-nine pump across the backside.

'You can fuck right off!' the nine-year-old Lamont yelled over his shoulder as he exited the school hall, never to return.

Now back at the car on this fine June day, we angle and lean our rods against the fence.

'Sorry,' I say, seeing that he's slightly cross at my open laughter. 'It's just the image of him tearing up your little bird club card, like being drummed out of the cavalry and having your sword broken in two across the general's knee while you're piped out of the fort. Did he snap your binoculars in half, too?'

He opens his car boot and plonks himself down inside, awkwardly wriggling out of his wading boots before breaking into a smile.

'Bob, the bastard,' he says, the trauma of revisiting his youth having obviously subsided. 'I loved that bird club – the feathery fuckwits.'

6
Naked Neon Fish Porn

Prepare yourself for some epically dark shit. Forget The Exorcist. Forget Saw. Forget The Audition. Forget Brexit. Forget Covid. Forget Trump and his rabid supporters. Forget Truss nose-diving one of the world's biggest economies into the ground, like a fucking dart, in just a shade under seventy-two hours. What I am about to roll for you is a front-loaded joint that will take you on a ferocious, hollow-tipped voyage of true terror. Your jaw will clamp, your teeth will grate down to the raw nerve, your eardrums will explode, your eyes will sew themselves shut and your bones will turn to powder. Some dark, dark shit this way comes, so gather your loved ones and hold them close, as chances are that you will never be quite the same again. Pour a large one and prepare to go over the top into a hailstorm of bullets, face-first towards a deadly blizzard of molten shrapnel.

The River Eden is one hundred miles north of my terraced house in Clitheroe. Catch figures for this river only reach me via cult-like secret winks and hushed tones; cloak-and-dagger tactics. My friends who fish the Eden would take a second to casually glance around the bar area before whispering its name. 'Not here, let's go in the back,' would be the boilerplate response in local boozers, said in a sober and sombre monochrome. Doe-eyed, I would follow after them, eager to receive the key to this mystery. Suddenly plunged into a gritty John Le Carre Cold War spy novel, Peter the retired upholster became George Smiley letting me in on sensitive classified material.

In angling, information is fuzzy and always puts you squarely in 'take with a pinch of salt' territory, so knowing when to pull the cord on distorted bullshit, parachute away from fiction and try to land on fact is essential. Embellished tales grow by the drained pint glass, usually correlative of the increasing time since a measurable success, which is why I try to think of the reggae tune Liquidator by the Harry J Allstars if an angler has me cornered. That way, I can filter any bunk information by not taking it seriously. Try it next time you're in any kind of meeting situation, and some bloated executive is talking at you while blocking your only line of exit.

Peter Smiley, upholsterer and spy, has all the info on the Eden circus. He is in the inner intelligence circle and knows where the bodies are buried. When the rivers Ribble and Lune were underperforming in the 1990s, Peter and his spirited group of visionary, pioneering pals went north, four to a car in a heroic effort to save on petrol, moving to a stealth theme from The Getaway by Lalo Schifren. What they discovered is the stuff of angling legend: they got into fish, lots of fish. Free-lined shrimp was his personal preference (think the fluid, sweeping dynamic brush strokes of Picasso and feel the funk flow), and in my last book, Hooked on Hope, I briefly mention some numbers. Without wanting to go over old ground, I will just say that on one particular day, back in the late nineties, four anglers hooked thirty-two salmon. Eventually, this glorious haul faded into the far distance of time, packed away inside the suitcase of legend, where it atrophied until it was nothing more than teary-eyed nostalgia. Twenty years later, as middle age gave way to chronic oldness, the painted sunshine of optimism was replaced by a weary dose of pessimistic cynicism, but Smiley's people didn't forget. Throughout twenty years of dreamy hindsight, they vowed that if ever the Eden picked up again, they would remain tight-lipped; no grapevine, no jungle drums and certainly zero social media. If the good times were going to roll again, it would be on a strictly need-to-know basis.

What happens in Carlisle stays in Carlisle and loose lips sink ships, so don't be a gob on stilts, eh?

As I mentioned all the way back in Chapter Two, an article appeared declaring that the Eden had rolled back the years and returned to form. It had melted the ball clean over the pavilion, and now ears all over the north of England were pricking up; even headstones in the graveyards twitched with ambition. After reading this article for myself, I phoned Peter, with whom, just for the sake of context, I have fished on numerous occasions over the last twelve years. He also upholsterers the period furniture that I attempt to sell, so it's safe to say that I spend quite a bit of time with Peter 'Sneaky Bastard' Smiley.

When I tell him about the article, he simply goes quiet. Then, after a considered pause of some length, he says in his slow East-Lancastrian drawl, 'Aye, it's been belting for a couple of years now. My mate had twenty-three last year. I had twelve, but I only went a few times. Where's this article?'

Utterly bewildered, and internally surging with a torrent of feelings ranging between surprise, betrayal and grudging admiration, I happily report that it's now national news; the wolves are at the door.

'Oh, bloody hell,' Peter 'Weasel' Smiley sighs.

Approximately thirty minutes later, I am a fully paid-up member of Carlisle Angling Association. Thirty minutes after that transaction, I am sat in the New Inn with Peter captive in the hot seat. Peter's Achilles heel is beer.

In the words of the Stereo MCs, it's time to get connected.

'I'm not allowed to say anything,' he insists, after one pint of White Witch.

Peter is fidgety. He rubs his hands and then briefly sits on them, perhaps hoping to stop his body language betraying him. Legs crossed, closed for business, he coyly looks around the snug to ensure that we are definitely alone. He shifts in his seat, I buy him a jumbo bag of Quavers, but still he won't crack. He starts trying to talk about football.

Bollocks to that.

While reading aloud from the article on the Eden, I highlight all the bullet points, each one a spectacular firework in its own right. As these verbal rockets pop and fizz, Peter deflects with an accusation against the author.

'Yeah, but who wrote it?' he asks. 'Probably some tool who doesn't know what he's on about. Could just be fake news.'

'It was written by the chairman of Carlisle Angling Association,' I answer calmly, but not without obvious enthusiasm. 'I would imagine he has a clue.'

What I want to do is bang my clenched fist on the table as I speak – you know, for dramatic effect – a la Richard Burton in Where Eagles Dare, that kind of thing; maybe slap him sharply across the face with a leather glove and kick him off his stool, but I fight this urge and instead suggest another pair of pints.

At the bar, I remind myself that Peter is in fact a friend of mine, rather than a Nazi paratrooper I had captured in a field behind Low Moor Club. I keep this in mind as I retake my seat opposite him.

'Are you enjoying those cheesy Quavers?' I ask. 'Is the tasty cold beverage to your liking?'

Jesus, I sound like Samuel L Jackson in Pulp Fiction.

Oh well, I'm too far in to abort now. I can see no recourse

other than to plough ahead and hope that some of this shit sticks; step hard or get stepped on. Peter looks confused, but he nods anyway. I judge that the second pint should be starting to kick in.

'Do you know what they call crisps in posh shops?' I resume the line of questioning.

He sheepishly shakes his head.

'Then I will tell you. They call them "artisan, fair trade, bespoke potato snacks," and do you know why they call them artisan, fair trade, bespoke potato snacks? They call them artisan, fair trade, bespoke potato snacks to give them a thinly-veiled sound of having green credentials. Now, Peter, I ask what would you call them?'

He seems energised and invigorated, his closed posture swinging open as he sits forward in the chair, feet uncrossed and then planted like fence posts on the pub floor. There is a fire behind his eyes; I have obviously touched a nerve as, downing the rest of his second pint in one, he wipes his mouth and erupts.

'Crisps!' he shouts. 'I'd call them crisps. They're just fucking crisps! Artisan producers, Artisan bakers – everything's fucking hand-crafted. Signature sausages! Ethical beekeeping! Scented candles, local bespoke cheeses that pack a culinary punch – does my fucking head in! We had all that in a single row of independent shops before the supermarkets took over, you know.'

It's going far better than I'd dared imagine. Peter has cracked like the glaze on an artisan antique pot; the artisan, fair trade, bespoke potato snacks have broken him. They've tasered him from his self-imposed silent censorship; there are no support groups to offer guidance to those suffering under the bombardment. For how long the poor man has been carrying this burden is anybody's guess.

Ordering two more pints, I dive headfirst into the Eden, and over the course of the following three rounds, a collage image of this most prolific river starts to take shape. He weaves a spellbinding tapestry of 4am starts and successful clandestine visits, in which each salmon lie is exposed and all fishing methods are explored; access points, pool names and rumours are at last confirmed.

Like the Hatton Garden heist, a loose plan begins to take shape.

Peter agrees that we will car share the one hundred miles up the M6 to Carlisle, where he will act as my guide, though as I mentioned in the opening chapter, these first forays to the Eden are destined to end in stone-cold disappointment.

Fool's gold? Well, it isn't the first time I've been sold a pup. For the last of our initial trips, he suggests we leave it until mid-June when, he assures me, with just the right set of conditions and a small dose of luck, I may hear a different melody.

It is June 21st, and I am outside Peter's house at 6am sharp. We have the fly rods in the car, but they're really just for pretend, as there's very little chance of them seeing the light of day. From June 16th, anglers are allowed to shrimp, so that's what we're going to do. Braid, slide a twenty-gram float to a weight and then swivel, followed by a fifteen-pound Maxima, shrimp pin and treble. In these conditions, the fly rod feels like an ugly haymaker at the end of an overelaborate dance, when what's really needed is a solid, heavy straight right down the centre.

On the drive up, Peter repeats some fantastic stories and anecdotes from the glory days, and also helps to fill in my internal crime board of recent events, as I get out the pins and red string to link all the shadowy usual suspects. In under two hours, we park up at the nearest access point for the Long Pool, leaving us half a mile away from the river. We get our gear on and march down the narrow farm track, and it occurs to me to tell Peter about my son's school hiring an inflatable assault course by way of a treat. The event is called the De-stresstival, at which we both laugh.

Skirting the woods at the bottom of the track, we find that in between us and the river stand two open fields and around fifty feisty heifers, all seemingly giddy as they skip about in the early-morning sunshine. Peter looks concerned, I pretend not to be, but my resolve is tested when, roughly thirty metres or so into the field, the heifers start to scamper over for a closer look at us. We keep going, and Hypothetical Peter (see book two) reminds that me he has two new knees. Upping my own pace, I call back over my shoulder to reassure him that he will be fine.

Admire the distance.

Back in 1978, when I was ten, my dad arrived home with four calves: three bulls and one cow. Did we live on a farm? No, so we had to keep them in an out-building (which wasn't even ours), and it became my job to muck them out and feed them. As a result of my feral upbringing, I have no fear of most animals, but I do have a healthy respect for what they can do when spooked or scared. I reared those bulls and the cow until they were too large for the out-building, at which point they suddenly vanished. My dad told me that they had gone to live in a lovely, lush green field somewhere, and naïvely – I've always been stupidly naïve – I believed him. It wasn't until Christmas Day 1993 that I found out what had really happened, after my mum, brother and sister all started laughing about how mental our household was, and I mentioned the fate of my bovine friends. My dad then informed us, right in the midst of the annual festive feast, how John, Paul and Ringo had been sold for meat, while Daisy had gone to live her best life in a lovely, lush green field, only to be struck by lightning and instantly incinerated.

'I thought you knew,' he concluded with a shrug.

Naïve. I've always been stupidly naïve.

Once I'm safely and smugly over the fence and on the riverbank, I encourage Peter to follow suit, all the while sounding like the bloke on the collapsed jetty in Jaws.

'Come on, Peter. Don't look back, just run!'

What to save first, his lunch or his gear? I wonder. Probably lunch. I already have loads of tackle.

Moving like a partly-broken Victorian clockwork toy, Peter finally reaches the fence and flings himself over with the urgent precision of a rodeo clown. Only now does he realise that the heifers lost interest with fifty metres to go.

That's entertainment.

He laughingly calls me a wanker, and we take a seat on a utilitarian, artisan, handmade wooden club bench overlooking the Long Pool. The time is 8.30am, and as we each pour a coffee and start to set up, there are no other anglers anywhere to be seen. This gives us much pleasure; arriving at your favourite spot only to find somebody else there is undeniably gutting, but for now at least, the river seems to be exclusively ours. The Long Pool on the River Eden is right by the M6 motorway, and much like its name suggests, it's long, wide and has an average depth of around four feet. The flow is slow and steady, glamorous it isn't. If anything, it's quite openly stark, like a plain brown envelope, and my bet is that its views have never featured in a landscape painting.

Seated high up on the bank, we have a clear view right down to the bend, a distance of maybe eight hundred metres. Roughly a quarter of the way down, there is a huge, overgrown concrete plinth that juts out into the river; the water is cold and clear. Peter and I have now had a brew and set up our shrimp rods, both electing to use twenty-gram sliding floats after judging the depth at somewhere between three and four feet. Then, as we finish our drinks, we see a spanking fresh salmon leap bodily right in front of us, before landing back in the slow mid-current with a loud splash. No sooner has this fist landed than another has leaped, not fifty metres to my left. Two more crashes one hundred metres below us – wait, three more! Each of these fish appears to be brand-new, fleetingly displaying their shining, metallic scales and majestic form in the early hue of a fresh-born day.

Peter gets in above me and casts out. I get in thirty metres below him, and as soon as my float lands, a salmon clears it. There are salmon leaping all over the Long Pool; we can't believe what we're seeing. The excitement needle is red-lining; this never happens, not like this; not in England, and especially not to me. Finding it hard to keep my shit together and not just scattergun cast at every moving fish, I remind myself to keep it line and length. Peter's float vanishes as he's into a salmon, so I wind in and get the net before slowly moving to his right shoulder. Fish are leaping everywhere, but Peter is unflappable as his target makes several long runs until eventually it's ready. The net is slipped under and it's in, and what a belter it is, fresh run and sea-liced, in the region of seventeen pounds. We shake hands and the fish is returned from whence it came.

'Get yourself in, Boo,' he says, practically beaming. 'We could get ten today. There's a good few fish just arrived, and they might be making themselves comfy for a while. Plus, they've stirred up the residents that were already here.'

On my next cast, my float is brutally buried by a fish, but I miss it. As I reel in to have another go, my phone rings. The caller is my wife Ams (Anne-Marie). The time is 9.25am.

'Peter's just had a cracker,' I enthusiastically state by way of answering, hoping it will let her know that my time is precious. 'There are fish everywhere.'

'Francis has had an accident,' she begins breathlessly, 'an ambulance is on its way. I'm walking to the school now. He was on a large inflatable assault course when another kid landed on his knee and dislocated it. His kneecap is around the back of his leg. You need to come home now while I go with him to the hospital.'

As I respond, still in shock from this dark magic, and simultaneously glancing at the river and Peter, it's with the vainest of hope that I seek definitive clarification.

'So, I should come home now, then. . .or should I get home for three?' I ask, thinking I could possibly get away with just collecting our daughter from school, before meekly adding, 'impact overlap?'

With extreme prejudice, my instructions are repeated beyond any doubt. Ams is a kind, patient person, full of love and care, but my enquiries have exasperated even her, as she confirms my departure time as: 'Immediately, now!'

Looking south, I can almost see the storm clouds generated by Ams's ire, and having intuitively read between the lines, I realise that now is not the greatest time to mention that I am neither a doctor nor an orthopaedic surgeon, or to ask if this situation really requires both of us. It's something the younger me would have definitely said, so I give this Boo version 5.4 a mental pat on the back for being so worldly and wise.

Meanwhile, the finest salmon I have ever seen are leaping all over in a psychedelic river mosaic motage.

Splash, splash. Leap, leap. Splash, bastarding splash.

This fucking so-called De-stresstival was an award for the way the kids had all handled lockdown. My teenage son Francis had been halfway through the inflatable course, in midroll after diving over a five-foot wall, when another kid landed on him with such force, it popped his knee out like a champagne cork.

Peter has been watching me on the phone. He's not daft, he's seen my face. He knows that something is up. I start to explain why we need to leave this rarest of opportunities, and he instantly agrees without issue.

'Family first,' he says sincerely. 'The poor lad.'

Externally, Peter appears to be fine, but as we all come to learn in life, looks can be deceiving. Internally, he is as dislocated as my son's knee, his wounded soul resembling one of Goya's black paintings. Looking at him, all I can see is Saturn Devouring His Son, and as we pack up and start climbing up the bank towards the bench, we subject ourselves to one more painful glance back at a paradise lost while slinging our bags over our shoulders. I fix my stare on the exact spot where a huge salmon around the mid-twenty-pound mark launched past me like a cruise missile in a twisting sideways vault before landing in an epic tsunami.

Lips pursed and shrivelling, we both just knowingly shake our heads, laugh and sigh, and by 9.35am, we are on our way back home, leaving nothing but broken dreams in our wake. During the two-hour drive, I speak to Ams. She tells me she could hear my son's screams of agony and distress from a hundred metres away, and how in order to rescue him, the plucky ambulance crew had to navigate the massive De-stresstival inflatable that took up most of the school yard.

Imagine that.

Francis Gilbraith made a full recovery. His father, meanwhile, is still working through his own personal trauma. He has been clinically diagnosed with PTSD (Post-Traumatic Salmon Disorder) and can be found wandering aimlessly along the backstreets of Clitheroe as he mutters the words, 'But they were everywhere!' over and over again.

Salmon Anonymous meet most Fridays in the snug of the New Inn, Clitheroe.

Honestly, they were everywhere. All over. Brand-new. EVERYWHERE!

7
Tangled Up in Boo

26th October 2021
Season status: blanking!

Having been all smiles at the start of the season, I am now starting to worry that I might blank. I know it's happened to better anglers than me, but for whatever reason, I've never gone through a whole season without a catch before, and I don't want to break that habit now. I'm determined that my season won't end up a skip fire, but as 31st October (close season) slides ever closer, I'm starting to twitch and feel cornered.

Now, I may come across like I have serenity all sewn up, but don't you fucking kid yourself. I may not need to catch 'em all, but I want to nab at least one. To me, the blank is a vulgar dark corridor, a hole in my soul, a void. Very immature, I know, and when the dark day finally arrives, of course I'll reluctantly take it on the chin, but until that happens, I will do everything in my power to swerve it. I've tied powerful, supernatural flies using carefully found and gathered feathers from magical birds, including ravens, magpies and jackdaws, and walked over Pendle Hill backwards with them all in my pocket while offering chants of praise to Terrence. Ceremonies have been performed before every lift, but not a pull has been felt nor a fin spotted.

Since taking voluntary redundancy from the cracker factory

in 2015, my career path has been one motorbike jump too many, a series of failed stunts, swimming against the flow in a seemingly ever-decreasing circle. My case file reads as follows: opened an antique shop (Lost and Found) then three years later, closed the antique shop; moved to a staffed retail rent-a-space at a large antique centre in Preston, but despite lumbering on as best I could, with another forty street-savvy antique dealers sharing the same building, it was only ever a brutal fight for a knife in the mud (not my scene). Finally, Covid arrived and made my mind up for me. My balloon was descending at an alarming rate, leaving me breathlessly blowing up into the gaping cavity in a desperate attempt to stay aloft. The writing was so clearly on the wall: economic freefall and a bloodbath for small businesses. Any dead weight had to be jettisoned, fat had to be trimmed, and believe me, there wasn't much of that. A tactical withdrawal took place, all the way back to my small unit in Clitheroe, where the business comprised of me, my van and my unit, operating under a model that became very fluid (i.e., hand-to-mouth and scheme-to-scheme).

Meanwhile, heavy rainfall has put the river out of commission, so I'm here in my unit, standing over a 6x3ft canvas while trying to make something from nothing. Since 2015, I have been selling my own abstract paintings, born mostly out of boredom and a necessity for original stock. I started hanging my own unsigned works in my shop, and just like with fishing, I simply waited to see what happened. On one occasion, a particularly elegant and sophisticated customer picked out two of my pieces from a gallery of around ten established artists and asked, 'Do you know who painted these?'

After explaining rather nervously that unfortunately I had no idea, I then added confidently that whomever the artist was, they had clearly been inspired by Mark Rothko.

'They obviously have great flair and passion,' the customer said with a nod.

'Those are my thoughts, too,' I replied.

That customer went on to buy four of my paintings. Gradually, I sold more, and even had two commissioned, so now, when all else fails, I paint.

And I bloody love it.

In my unit, I have a vintage Sharp VZ 2000 boombox that I hook up to my iPod, and as I paint, dance and sing to a playlist, I feel very free. Vibrant, honest energy intertwines with joy, pain, happiness and sadness; my work is always spontaneous, never quite knowing which direction it will go in is very much part of the buzz. Sometimes, it's a case of capturing topics like monotony, or it can just be abstract landscapes of places where I've been fishing; moments, memories and emotions are all one with the notes and strokes; energy transferred and reshaped.

The abstract painting I've been working on for over a week is taking shape. It's been done to the tune of Run the Jewels' brand of belligerent hip-hop, along with a more sedate track, Hard Times, by Baby Huey. Hard Times on repeat for six or more plays, wearing a Star Trek engineer's paint-spattered boilersuit. I'm off-grid, nobody knows where my unit is. I don't want visitors, I want to be totally tangled up in Boo. At the same time, my eye is on the clock because the river will be dropping in nicely, and with more rain forecast to be on the way, my window of opportunity is narrowing fast. One more decent lift of water and it's game over for the season. Time to let the paint dry and get myself to another arresting realm.

Only ten minutes from home and all quiet on the club car park, as I hurriedly get my waders and gear on. With my beloved Barbour (I'm no longer sure who is wearing who) and a net slung over my back, I have three boxes of flies, one spool of mono, forceps and scissors, and a thirteen-foot Vision Catapult already set up. Everything I am using belonged to somebody else at one point, all the way down to my odd wading boots. One is a (borrowed) Greys, the other a Simms whose partner's felt sole fell victim to the Ribble and peeled off. The afternoon is lit up as I stroll across the fields to the river, accompanied by my tackle ghosts, music playing in my ear buds (Pokey LaFarge is urging me to get it 'fore it's gone). My mood is elevated by the prospect of another roll of the dice, and as I scoot through a stream and head for pool named Jona's, I find it at a near perfect height.

As usual, there is only me on. To my left is Pendle Hill, cast in silver under a wisp of softly-spoken cloud, and then turning yellow as the sun breaks through and highlights all its scars, time-pressed and eroded by pressure. The run I am in is stunning, framed by willow trees on the far bank dipping the tips of their drooping branches into the pushing water. The flow is perfect, the run is long, and once I'm in, I can fish without stopping for a good two hundred metres. The bottom of the pool is signified by one of our huts, and after wading three-feet deep, I hug a bank that's shrouded by long meadow grass and reeds. Here, Pendle Hill almost feels like it's on top of me, like a recumbent ancient monolith, and having decided that this is the run to fish, my aim is to go through twice.

The first run through takes nearly two hours. At the hut, I give it twenty minutes and then leg it back to the top and start again. No fish have shown as I'm slowly making my way around the first bend, demonstrating my season in a nutshell: an endless slew of broken promises. My Alan Shearer stoat's tail is on my dropper and my own tied Witch's Boo (you know, instead of brew) raven fly is on point. Looking at Pendle, I mutter a heartfelt plea through gritted teeth.

'Come on, ladies,' I urge. 'Come on, Terrance. Come on, Ahab.'

Convincing myself that my sink tip is sinking too fast, I make the switch to a ten-foot intermediate and cast. This feels better, and with my playlist now on to Lithium by the Polyphonic Spree, the line 'I'm so happy coz today I found my friends, they're in my head,' has me smiling from ear to ear. I make a cast to the far bank, and almost instantly a salmon hits the fly. Slowly lifting into it, it takes line and steals deep. The Polyphonic Spree is in full flow, the fish is going on a proper run, and because my reel has no clutch, I have to use my thumb on the spool to slow its pace ahead of a great big head shake, a full-blown belly roll and another run. Marc E Smith is now snarling and telling me how he lost his temper with a friend, as his band the Fall play Dr Buck's Letter, and, winding in, I slowly gain ground on what has turned out to be a large coloured cock fish. A stalemate ensues as I get over the fish with a short line; the water is heavy and the bank is steep, and looking all around me, I realise there's nowhere to bank the fish. Left-handed, I get the net off my back and, placing its head under my left boot, extend it out. Three times we dance with me failing to net it, until it's fourth time lucky and I get the fish in.

Un-fucking-believable! Where the hell did that come from? What surrealist's palette could produce such alchemy? At first, my glad eye thought it was a twenty-pounder, but seeing it in the net, I concede to myself that it's more in the region of sixteen or seventeen. Whatever the case, the fish doesn't leave the water; holding it while waiting to feel it kick and go was just magical, the culmination of so much effort, joy and love. The happiness coursing through my body must have me looking luminous, lit up like a thermal image on a satellite photo.

Energy transferred.

Mission accomplished, I trot back to the car park like it's The Greatest Show on Earth and replay Lithium in an attempt recapture the initial brain explosion. Everything is better now.

Obviously, I send all my weary blanking mates my good news, and then I phone Lamont to tune him into my good fortune. He is, as always, surprised, as he patronisingly tells me, 'Well done, you,' before very quickly changing the subject from me to something slightly more obscure. 'Do you know that bloke who's recording all the fish? He's weeks away from finding out what they're talking about.'

That night at home, Ams and I celebrate. A game of two halves: half a space cake each and half a bottle of red wine, kitchen disco. From my back door, Pendle Hill is clearly visible, and I realise that something feels out of balance. Raising a toast doesn't seem to be enough of a gesture; this has not been a solo effort. From the found feathers donated by the birds and the ghosts of my gear, to my desperate plea for help, an equilibrium must be returned. Days like this don't just happen, they must be conjured.

As Lithium plays, we honour the day by burning the fly that had caught the fish. After all, if it wasn't skill, it must have been witchcraft.

8
Fifty Miles of Lies

Clue Number One: the Inn at Whitewell

As if finding a willing salmon wasn't an engaging and arduous challenge enough!

Most mature adults will no doubt think of a quest as some form of cleansing self-improvement exercise, or a laborious path to a deeper understanding or even growth; maybe a career leg-up or financial security leap that improves their quality of life, or perhaps even a spiritual pathway to a broader sense of true enlightenment; something so righteous, it guides them all the way to the glittering disco ball of wisdom and knowledge.

Like I said, mature adults.

When Lamont and I find out that we have unexpectedly been chosen to participate in a quest, we both simultaneously picture the same heady scene: Jason and the Argonauts searching for the golden fleece.

Treasure!

We are in the windowless back room of the New Inn, Clitheroe, having a swift couple of pints while outlining the travel arrangements for our forthcoming Spey trip. We like the windowless box of a back room because nobody can see you in there; they can't rat you out for being momentarily free. The pub attracts a steady stream of customers, just enough daytime traffic to keep it passively ticking over. Nothing ever seems to change at the New Inn, no fashion fads or sudden price hikes. It radiates a subtle, pure honesty, and is certainly not trying to impress anybody; no Emperor's New Clothes here, not in this rare oasis in a world that's trying too hard to be liked. So, if you haven't guessed already, the New Inn's belligerence towards the marketing sales pitch of change means that we like it a lot. There are always a few intriguing wrung-out barflies stuck to the invisible fly paper of the pub bar, whose much-aired world insights could have given Charles Bukowski a run for his money, and on this particular Friday afternoon in March, the place seems more dimly lit and slightly darker than usual. In the absence of natural light, the open fire crackles and flickers into life, its flames providing a warm theatrical ambiance, and we both sit facing it while sharing a round Britannia bar table and two pints of Moorehouse's Pride of Pendle. That's when Quint glides in as if on skates.

Quint is a tall, lean, athletic and very tanned man in his early seventies. Dressed in grey skinny-fit chinos, Chuck Taylor All-Star high-top Converse trainers and a faded white tour T-shirt bearing the Free lyric 'All right now,' an ensemble framed by a blue-cotton French chore jacket that has an admirable charismatic washed-out patina, he looks much younger than he really is. According to his now deceased brother Ahab, Quint retired aged fifty-five after thirty years working as an engineer at Rolls Royce, making off with a super-charged, diamond-encrusted pension that afforded him the ability to migrate south every winter for the last twenty years. Moderation has obviously been his mantra; the kind of guy who is dipped in gold and always gets a better deal than you. Quint cycles, golfs, fell walks and eats clean, all by choice. His retirement plan was the perfect blueprint: happy, healthy and making the most of it. Possessing close to an incredible one hundred percent mobility, all his own teeth and a full head of white hair, he's a real Saga pinup poster boy. As an angler, however, he is the type that will only go when somebody else has already done all the legwork and told him there are a few fish about. He wants all the information, but he lacks the inclination to dig in and find it for himself; it's just where, what and when. In this respect, it helped having a brother like Ahab, a man who lived for the cycle of the season and was joined at the hip to the river. Quint can fish, to be fair to him, and he has a warm personality that just about masks an ultra-competitive nature. He is also piously fly-only, and he displays a methodical elegance when spotted in a pool, so it'll probably come as no surprise that Lamont and I both much preferred his brother. Privately, we refer to Quint as the 'captain of the yacht club,' while he considers us to be toeing the fine line between outright deadbeat dossers and dangerous idiots.

That's not a true, I am self-celebrating!

Quint never thinks about us for longer than one hundredth of a second, if it's even as much as that – he's far too busy winning at life – hence our bemused glances when he pulls up a seat at the table and slides me a cream-coloured, sealed manila envelope.

'He could be a funny old bird,' he says, tapping the envelope.

While wondering how Quint knew where to find us, I open the letter contained within and read its contents aloud.

My time is slipping away and I know it. My life cycle is coming to an end. It is time for me to make my run upstream. Nature dictates that if you're not growing then you're dying, so I've made preparations for my journal, Fifty Miles of Lies, to survive.

In its pages are the true locations of every lie I ever caught a salmon from on the Ribble. Fifty years of knowledge. Fifty years of graft. My life's work documented with great detail and subtle thoughts. Having spent time with you two jokers, it became all too apparent that you need all the help you can get.

BE WARNED! This journal must be earned. It will not be a quick win. This quest isn't for the faint-hearted or the time-strapped. I buried it alongside the Ribble, somewhere between Preston and Clitheroe. Your first clue can be found under an armchair inside the Inn at Whitewell. Follow the clues and get the book. You just might learn something along the way.

Play-happy,
Ahab

'Be warned!' Lamont scoffs, looking at me and rolling his eyes. 'That's a bit Treasure Island, isn't it? He might as well have added a "fare-ye-well."'

Quint smiles, and all three of us start to laugh at the thought of Ahab grinning as he wrote this letter. For me, it ignites a warm, cheerful and nostalgic moment; briefly, I can see his lean, wind-worn face again, his tanned features highlighted by a dappled spring sunshine; his gye net on his back and his rod on his shoulder as he looks out over the river he loved so much. Obviously, we're thrilled to be given this challenge from the afterlife; the spectre of Ahab has reached out to place a ghostly hand on our shoulders, offering a welcome adventure as we creep down the slender hallway of life.

Or maybe it's a penance?

Lamont and I agree to wait a few weeks before beginning this mammoth task. Buy the ticket, take the ride. Sun rises, sun sets, with life happening in between.

Some weeks after receiving Ahab's letter from beyond, we

find ourselves in the front bar of the Inn at Whitewell, situated in the Forest of Bowland on the banks of the River Hodder. The place is old, almost ancient, with character and charm running through its veins, its bones full of stories both told and untold. The original manor house dates back to the fourteenth century, long before it became another pub that's joyously slow on progress, featuring comfortable, well-used antique furniture and rich, handmade rugs across worn flag floors, and walls adorned with an array of sporting artworks. It's a style of décor accurately described online as country, traditional and warm. We are immediately happy in these diamond-cut surroundings. Pints are pulled and we seat ourselves on an eighteenth-century oak settle that faces the bar.

'What now?' a smirking, shrugging Lamont says.

He fumbles around blindly under the bench we are sat on, while I scan the room for a likely hiding spot. There is an elegant, comfortable-looking, tweed-covered wingback chair marinating in the corner of the bar area, and from its vantage point you can see the entire bar.

Ahab would have liked that, I think.

Casually, I walk over to inspect the wingback, only to 'accidentally' drop my car keys and kick them under it as I approach. This draws a sigh of 'Oh, Jesus,' from Lamont, but ignoring this, I tilt the chair backwards and look underneath. Amazingly, there I find an envelope stuffed into the webbing of the upholstery. I quickly grab it and scuttle back to our bench where, clumsy and nervous, I place it on the table. Judging by its crumpled, stained appearance, it's very apparent that this envelope had been reused, but our names are clearly visible on the front, written in green ink. We share a glance as I slowly peel it open.

Hello boys!

I backed against you getting this far – the beginning. Well done! Adversity is the parent of virtue.

The pub is fantastic, isn't it? The pool behind it was mustard for sea trout in the eighties. 11.55pm, 9th June 1987. Let me take you back.

The grass was damp and fresh with recent light rain. Long, lean and searching for life-giving sunlight, it was one of those evenings where you feel tuned in and turned on, nature's complex overture as a soundtrack, a contradiction as it simultaneously felt so quiet yet as busy and vibrant as any major city. Darkness took forever to arrive. 10 minutes in, and I start to hear some large splashes. My eyes had adjusted to the lack of light – the 9'6" rod was set up with a dry line and an 8ft cast. 4ft of 12lb line to 4ft of 10lb mono. I wanted to fish sub-surface, so added Mucilin quick-sink to the leader. On my short dropper, I had on a Harold Howorth Blae and Black size-10, and on point I had a size-8 tandem Medicine on. This set-up was my favourite in the dark.

Wading into the river, I was low and slow. Knee-deep, I made my first cast across the pool. After a slow 40 minutes, I was through the pool. There was a decent fish in there, I could hear it plain as day. Sitting out for 20 minutes, I started again. On my third cast, the rod was almost jolted from my grasp as a massive fish cartwheeled through the air – cowboy rodeo job! Hanging on for grim death, I start backing up, but as I did, I slipped on my arse backwards into the drink. The fish got a second wind and went for the stars again. Gathering myself, I got back on my feet soaking wet, the rod vibrating in my hands until eventually I felt in charge. My heart was banging like Thumper's foot as I dragged the fish into the shallows and banked it on an elevated tuft of exposed grass. Quickly, the bugger was chapped then unhooked – Harold's Blae and Black had done the job. 9lb 40z, easily the biggest sea trout I ever caught. I never bettered it, despite spending the rest of my life trying to replicate that magical moment of blissful ciaos.

Now then, boys, it's time for another. Get yourselves to the stables at the Aspinall Arms, Mitton. In the third bay, there's a copper planter. Take a good look at it.

Don't trade love for money,
Ahab

'It's Ahab's greatest hits!' Lamont exclaims. 'The cheeky get.'

We move outside to a balcony platform overlooking the very pool we have just been reading about. Folding the letter up and placing it in my inside pocket, I ask Lamont if he thinks Ahab had been a member of the club that owns this beat. He takes in half his pint, and as a trout jumps in the pool, he sighs.

'No chance at all,' he says. 'Definitely Chinese airspace.'

Smiling, I give a knowing nod in complete agreement, as the pilot light on my inner glow ignites.

We take our time finishing our drinks, just to soak up the pleasure of each other's company and the marvellous lyrical ambiance of the place. Now that we know what our adventure entails, we are fully on-board and readily agree to meet at the Aspinall Arms in May, by which time we'll have returned from our River Spey trip in April. We then discuss the nature of solitude as explored in Henry David Thoreau's Walden, and how the modern equivalent of building an isolated log cabin in the woods is to unplug your wi-fi and switch off your phone, performing a virtual vanishing act.

Clue Number Two: National Anthems

Arriving at the Aspinall Arms in good time, I take the short stroll to the bridge and look downstream while waiting for Lamont. This is a happy place for me; my friend Matt Evans and I started a small festival here in 2011. We called it Cloudspotting, named for our love of daydreaming, and although we had no capital behind us, we somehow made it happen. A farmer let us use the field parallel to the river as a campsite, and we built a stage in the Aspinall's very large beer garden. Friends old and new attended, to be entertained by twenty-seven artists and bands, and it was all very exciting and heart-warmingly beautiful. Matt died in 2021, breaking lots of hearts in the process, including mine. He was the only person in my world who would have ever agreed to ride that cerebral roller coaster; the Cloudspotting story would make a great book, maybe one day. In the meantime, I say with the greatest reverence that I will be eternally grateful for all that Matt did. The guy was lit by a wry, dry, playful sense of mischief, and I will never forget him or our many musical adventures.

Looking downstream and across at the field we used, I vividly remember the time we had to remove six acres of sheep shit by hand before inviting our campers on-site. Naturally, Matt and I called upon our amazing wives to help, and as I grin at the thought of his smiling face and of us all laughing as we undertook the grottiest, most surreal of jobs, I let out an involuntary sob and start to cry. This impromptu outburst ends with a sigh as I wipe my face and pull myself together on the walk back to the pub, tucking it all away in the shadows for another day; shutting the grief monster back in its box.

The sun rises, the sun sets.

Inside the pub, I find a red leather chesterfield wingback next to the fire, on which I nurse a pint and await the arrival of Lamont. It isn't long before he's walking in and casing the joint while asking for a beer. He's dressed in his black work wear (more pockets than a snooker hall), and, giving me a nod of acknowledgement, he heads my way and says loudly, 'Our national anthem is shit. Have you heard the Welsh and the French? They make your sodding hair stand on end.'

He plonks himself down next to me in a leather club chair, and I'm automatically jolted from my melancholic grief funk.

'What would you suggest as replacement, then?' I ask.

'I don't know,' he says, rubbing the arms of the chair and stretching backwards, 'fucking anything. Imagine by John Lennon. Ain't Got No, I Got Life by Nina Simone. Do You Realize?? by the Flaming Lips. Twat by John Cooper Clarke. Everyday People by Sly and the Family Stone. Mr Pharmacist by the Fall. . .anything! Queens, kings and United Kingdoms. . .it's like we live in a children's fairy tale.'

Nina Simone, the Flaming Lips and John Cooper Clarke all instantly make my newly-activated national anthem chart. I'd watch miles more medal ceremonies if our winning relay team were proudly belting out Twat by JCC in the rarefied air of the top podium.

'Like a recently disinfected shithouse. . .'

Following Ahab's instructions, we walk across a wide tarmacked car park to the pub's outbuildings, where sure enough, there in the open third bay is a large copper planter. We give the target the full three-sixty search, but no envelope.

'Maybe it's underneath?' I say cautiously.

Tilting the planter backwards, we see the corner of an A5 envelope visible from inside a clear plastic sandwich bag.

'Fucking beautiful mad bastard,' Lamont laughs, shaking his head as he retrieves the next clue.

Back in a secluded corner of the pub, via the bar to collect two fresh pints, we open our latest prize. This time, it's Lamont's turn to read aloud. He stands for added dramatic effect.

Greetings!

One day soon, you will realise that your past is much longer than your future. Cling on to the fun times, wring out every moment. Don't fade on the bend, boys. Drive for the line.

On this beat, there are four spots you ALWAYS need to cover. For now, I will tell you about one, Hodder Foot, where the Hodder empties into the Ribble. Some pool, slow and deep, and full of mystery. . .

At this point, Lamont breaks off and rolls his eyes at Ahab's corny sense of scene setting. We both agree that the use of 'full of mystery' had been an error, and then Lamont returns to his performance. In his head, he is illuminated in a spotlight while reciting Richard III at the Old Vic.

. . .The river had been up about 14" and the colour was just starting to drop away. The year was 1989, fish had been holed-up on the lower river for a good few weeks. The bottom end had been peppered – yours truly had caught 12 in three days, all on the shrimp, and now I fancied a runner on the fly. The river had gone from an almost static summer level to an energised moving life force. The lift in water level meant that Hodder Foot would have enough flow to take a small copper tube fly on a full floating Spey line. It was about 2 o'clock in the afternoon and, using an old 15ft Bruce and Walker fly rod, I started to fish the left-hand bank down into Hodder Foot. Nobody else there, my black-and-silver tube was going out nicely. I reckon it was fishing about 2ft down as I casted square to fish it more like a spinner. Halfway down the pool, a fish hits it and runs downstream, staying deep. Slow power – really slow, heavy power. Knowing I was into a big fish, I backed out of the water and began to quietly follow it

downstream. *The banking was clear for about 200 yards. This fish was full fat, taking me to the tail of the pool twice before I could get enough line back to walk it upstream. For 30 minutes, I stayed on it. It was so big, you could hear it swimming! I was worried about my line and my knots, hoping the hook would hold firm – welcome to the Terrordome! In the centre of the pool, it comes up and thrashes the surface, massive violent head shake and tail slap. Its tail looked like a bloody shovel! It dived deep and surged downstream, all I could do was keep the pressure on and stay in touch while it ragdolled me. Finally, I got it on its side, gleaming fresh and 1ft-deep. Towing it up the gravel bank and flinging my rod as I dived onto it, my scales only went up to 30lbs and this fish bottomed them, so maybe 35?*

When you think the river's got its hands around your throat, remember the 'what if?' That's why we go. Dream big and dream often.

The next letter is taped under the pool table in the White Bull in Ribchester.

Kill time without injuring eternity,
Ahab

Lamont's impressive and vivid reading moves me as I process the story I've just heard.

'Do you think he put it back?' I ask rhetorically.

Lamont's eyebrows nearly fire off the top of his head as he excitedly responds, 'Nineteen eighty-nine! Over thirty pounds! There's more chance of us two building a time machine that actually works than repeating that catch.'

This reference to our younger days makes me burst out laughing, as Lamont, now laughing himself, continues.

'A double wardrobe, an alarm clock and a car battery all

wired together is not a time machine.'

Now I remember it clearly. Early nineties, fifteen dried magic mushrooms each, plus beers and some essential herbs, real high. We had wanted to go back in time and put some bets on to beat the bookmakers, nothing more ambitious than that. An hour later, two laughing twenty-somethings are stood inside a wardrobe with a clock radio set for the week before. Ten. . .nine. . .eight. . .seven. . .six. . .five. . .four. . .three. . .two. . .one. . .Shazam! Two laughing twenty-somethings exit the wardrobe and space walk past the terraced houses to the bookies, still laughing all the way, only to find that their time machine was just a wardrobe wired to a car battery, leaving them disappointingly stuck in the present. The two time travellers then laughed all the way to the pub.

Lamont puts his laughing head on mine, squeezes me and says, 'Fuck me, we had some fun. I proper love you, man.'

Head nodding, my eyes water at the sudden thought of hundreds of shiny, happy moments shared.

'Who loves ya, baby?' I reply with a smile. 'Ribchester next Wednesday?'

Clue Number Three: Remember Not to Forget

Spinning the eight ball as I remove the triangle, we toss a coin to decide who gets to break. Lamont always calls heads, I always go tails. We are in the White Bull in Ribchester, and Ahab's third letter has been retrieved from the underside of the pool table, ready to be read upon the conclusion of this frame of pool.

The White Bull is another old pub. The building has been here since 1707; there are the remains of a Roman bathhouse behind the beer garden. The pillars outside the main entrance, which elevate a borderline pagan wooden carving of a white bull, are from the Roman temple to Minerva and were salvaged from the Ribble, which runs past the village. Located at the convergence point of Roman roads from York, Chester and Carlisle, the Romans built a fort here in 70ad that was held by Spanish and later Samaritan cavalry for over four hundred years, and now our fearless adventurers, Lamontus Irrationalus and Boous Simpleus, have passed through these ancient pillars of dedication to the goddess of wisdom and are about to read a letter from a dead guy regarding a quest for a book about fish.

Stick that in your Roman museum.

With Lamontus now vanquished on the field of felt, we retire to the beer garden and lean against the wall, peeping over at the remains of the bathhouse.

'Ancient shit that,' Lamont declares, pointing at the ruins with one hand while clutching Ahab's letter in the other. 'Imagine being stationed here, with all the glory of the Roman Empire to go at. Poor fuckers, freezing their arses off in the middle of nowhere.'

It's a fair point. Their aspirations must have been for a Mediterranean posting, with Ribchester very much the grubby, cold and damp short straw.

'Spare me the in-depth history lesson,' I grin. 'Just read the letter.'

He opens the envelope and starts to read, probably imagining himself addressing the entire Roman senate.

Ow Do,

Keep swimming, boys, you're nearly there. I know you're both familiar with the pool known as Mort's. With 8" of water on in August, 2 days after a decent lift it's a dream to fish on the fly. Fish the bend for 40 yards before going down to the bottom. August is usually when the grilse arrive.

It's 1998, and using the river as my panacea, I headed for Mort's. Ubi amor, ibi dolor – some mistakes leave deep scars, so make sure you tell those that matter how much you care, how much you love them. Cultivate love, and life naturally follows.

Stood in the head of Mort's that day, I was conflicted. My head was twisting in the wind. One week earlier, I had heard that a former partner had got married. A small part of me had dreamt of a reconciliation. When I was given an ultimatum of them or the river, I had chosen the latter. Sometimes, regrets creep in. They seem to have their own haunting season, usually during the dark nights of the winter months, where they can lurk around in the shadows. . .

'Was he ever married?' Lamont breaks off to ask, taking the words right out of my mouth.

'I don't know,' is all I can offer, paired with a shrug. 'It never came up in conversation. We were always caught up in the moment of there and then. I wonder what the Latin means, *Ubi amor, ibi dolor?'*

'Where there is love, there is pain,' he answers, looking very pleased with himself as he looks off mystically into the distance, the gobshite.

I'm not having that! There is no effing way he knew it off the top of his head. Somehow, he has looked it up on his phone without me noticing. Lamont the Latin scholar? Not a chance. My head is still concentrating on deducing what the word 'panacea' means when I place my hand on his shoulder.

'Proceed with the letter reading,' I say quietly. 'I'm not sure how you knew what that Latin phrase meant, but I know that you didn't just know it, and I also know that you know you never knew. This perceived worldly intelligence you like to project is gossamer-thin. You're no throbbing intellect.'

'Due to my lofty intellectual position and addiction to cultural pursuits,' he closes his eyes for effect, 'I will choose to ignore those last bigoted remarks. Now, if I may be allowed to continue. . .'

. . . With my head in bits, I started down Mort's looking for a distraction. The needle was jumping on the scratched vinyl of my mind, with memories and moments, regrets and doubts on repeat. What was needed was a sudden knock to jump the needle to a new tune.

The water looked like black gloss, as the August sunshine cast a beam of light that broke through the clouds to highlight the woods' gentle community, which seemed to vibrate under the warming glow. Making a double Spey cast, I cast my fly at a 45-degree angle and gave the line a kind mend, just to slow the fly down. Halfway down the pool and casting into the wooded far bank, my black shrimp double is hit. Lifting into it, the water erupts and a lively grilse all of 5lbs launches into the air. It makes 2 runs before I net it. 4 more casts, and in the tail of the pool I hook and land another at about 8lbs.

With my head temporarily jolted off repeat, I saunter down to the bottom of the beat. The club had made a simple bench at the base of the tree, a nice place to sit and stop – to be. Sitting down, I had a coffee and thought about changing my fly. I didn't bother, though. I just checked my knot and had 5 minutes. There are 2 lies below the tree, about 30 feet apart. Staying as near to the bank as I could, I covered the 1st lie. Wham! straight away. Another grilse shoots across the river into the thinner water. I turn the fish, it runs downstream. Landed, it's about 6lbs, a hat-trick! Carrying on to the 2nd lie, I go through and expect a take. Nothing. So, wading out of the water and plodding up on to the bank, I go back to the 1st.

Casting above the lie, I try to angle my fly to go past slightly in front of where the last fish took. Something nips the fly, and then a second later the fish takes and piles quickly downstream. This fish has a more solid thump – deeper power, my click-and-pawl reel shouting its throaty song as my rod bounced under the pressure of the fish. After a tussle, I land a beautiful 11lbs salmon. 3 casts later, another grilse at 6lbs. An hour after that, I land a 6th fish. This last grilse was 8 or 9lbs.

6 salmon on the fly in 4 hours of perfect madness!

Had the cosmos reached out to me? Only time would tell.

What's a life without a few mistakes?

The next and final letter is in a biscuit tin under a plant pot in the back garden of the Bay Horse. I'm sure Lamont will know where.

Remember not to forget,
Ahab

'While we're both here, I think it's only right that we have a wander down,' I suggest, as we both automatically start out towards Mort's pool.

'I'm sure Lamont will know where,' Lamont says solemnly. 'He's sharper than flint, even when he's dead.'

I know instantly what the deceased Ahab is referring to, and I can imagine him laughing while writing that cheeky line. Don't worry, the story won't go untold, but I may as well let that seed germinate a little until we get to the last letter.

The bottom of this beat is where Ahab had passed away. Neither of us had been down there since, it just hadn't seemed right. Now, though, it felt like a poignant moment since, in a way, Ahab himself had asked us to go.

Climbing the stile and crossing eighty or so yards of lush

green farmland to the bank, we pass the plaque to Mort. He was before our time. You have to fish a spot with an obsessive frequency to have it named after you.

#Goals

Lamont and I slowly make our way down the bank, noting all the landmarks on the far side that remind us of our own past fishing encounters here. While merrily recounting successes and failures alike, he casually offers me a piece of trivia about death.

'Do you know, if you leave your body to medical science, they come and pick it up for free? Free!' He says this with a broad smile spreading across his face. Free is his favourite price. 'No funeral costs, nothing. They just whisk you away.'

Funnily enough, I've been giving funeral costs more storage space between my ears than normal recently. Must be an age thing.

By way of response, I reveal to him my own hypothetical funeral plan. Instead of an expensive coffin, I want to be cremated in a rolled-up carpet. Surely, it's better for the environment to kill two birds with one stone. Plus, I mean, imagine being carried aloft by your mates. One final comedy caper.

Lamont is visibly excited by the mental image.

'Would you be unrolled straight into the furnace?' he asks.

'In a perfect world, yes. That would be a definite crowd pleaser, one final flourish with plenty of room for error. . .'

I tail off without completing the thought, as I'm now deliberating over Lamont's medical science suggestion. As we walk on, I share my conclusion.

'I've heard some intriguing stories regarding medical students and cadavers,' I say, 'like one about a disembodied arm being stuck in the sleeve of a jacket, and then used to wave at people from the top deck of a bus.'

I can't quite tell if Lamont is grimacing or holding back a smile as he answers wryly, 'Public transport is to be avoided at all costs. What would you be charged with, bodysnatching? That would put you in an elite group, like them types who campaign for real ale. Imagine joining a group that campaigned for beer.'

We have arrived at the wooden seat near the tree that Ahab referred to, feeling all the wiser for this stimulating conversation. The simplicity and common beauty of this venerated place is astonishing; the river runs from shallow, white, fizzing and broken to black as ink where it ascends to slower-paced, deeper water (you could easily hide a baby elephant in some of the holes). The bench is part of the tree, and the tree is part of the bench. Somebody has even screwed a coat hook into its broad trunk.

We sit side by side and look down at the river flowing left to right, reading the letter aloud again in Ahab's bestowed account, better able to picture the scene as we observe the set. Here, the river is no longer Baby Bear, having grown up to become full-blown Daddy Bear; broad and boulder-strewn, with both calm and fast runs, less than one mile from the village, but oozing with the sensation that you are in a remote place. We sagely gesture to the first lie and then presume to know the second, both agreeing that it's a great place to cast a long line on a fly rod. There's plenty of room, good for either left hand up or if, like me, you prefer to double Spey cast, since space is not an issue.

No wonder he loved this place, I think. No wonder the Romans stayed on for so long.

Slowly walking back towards the village while skirting the riverbank, we have some normal conversations about our families and work, and as we discuss these ever-present issues that stalk us all like the Great Wave of Kanagawa by Katsushika Hokusa, our route is punctuated by stone-skimming competitions and distance stone throwing. The overall sense of calm is palpable, such that Lamont suggests we should pass through the pillars of Minerva more often.

During this amble, I can't help but think that maybe Ahab's quest was not just a simple treasure hunt. Maybe there was something else he wanted us to find, something about life; something about time; something about friendship; small empires and palaces, delving deep into the metaphorical.

After another quick pint, we agree to meet a week later to finish what Ahab started. Find the book, become superstar anglers and kiss the lean times goodbye forever. Think positive! In the pub car park, Lamont hands me a small bag of Bury black pudding.

'I have a contact,' he explains. 'I can't eat it fast enough.'

Having a person on the inside is prime currency. A black pudding here, a plate meat pie there, maybe even a dozen eggs. We don't deal in secret back-handed million-pound government contracts up here, but we know all the angles for Bury black puddings.

Clue Number Four: the White Picket Fence

Collecting Lamont from his Waco-inspired walled compound, it's obvious that he's as excited as I am. The car is full of fine vintage pop, as we try to sing along with Jacques Dutronc's classic Et moi, et moi, et moi, followed by Joe Jackson's Is She Really Going Out with Him? and with the summer evening energy radiating through us, there's a palpable sense of adventure in the air. Lamont is lively as he outlines his plan ahead of an upcoming interview for a new position, laying it all out as we close in on our target destination.

'When, at the end of the interview, they ask me if I have any questions for the panel, I will casually say yes and ask, "If you were an apple, what type of apple would you be?" Then, whatever their response, I will just look at them and say, "Really? That's very interesting." Turn the tables on 'em.'

He gives a knowing, satisfied nod to the tune of Barbra Streisand's Don't Rain On My Parade, which considering the situation is decent advice.

'That's genius,' I tell him, prompting another nod and a smile as we turn into the car park.

The Bay Horse is situated near Mellor and Osbaldeston, a central point between two beats on the Ribble, Sunderland Hall and Osbaldeston Hall. If you land in the Bay Horse at four in the afternoon following a stolen day on the river, there's a fair chance you'll bump into a few like-minded souls and perhaps become the beneficiary of some cheap group therapy.

Exiting the car, Lamont looks wistfully at the white picket fence that skirts the bottom of a nicely maintained beer garden. Smiling to myself, I say nothing.

'Don't say a word,' is all he says, as we go into the bar and order a pair of pints.

Lamont asks for a pint of Bearded Pony, and we hope there's no such thing as Bearded Pony. When the puzzled barman tells us that they don't have any Bearded Pony, I ask him for a pint of Roofer's Slipper, and we hope there's no such thing as a pint of Roofer's Slipper. Again, the barman regrets to inform us that they don't stock it, and all we can do is exchange shrugs of disappointed resignation.

'Two of those, then, please,' Lamont points at a beer pump.

This name game is one of our favourites, serving as an antidote to the boom in utter marketing sizzle surrounding beers and their exotic handles.

Small gains, tiny triumphs.

Secretly, I would quite like a pint of Salmon Weasel.

It's a bright, warm evening, so we go out into the beer garden. Examining our surroundings, we see there is indeed an overturned plant pot by a disused picnic table, in what is clearly a little-used, neglected corner. We're the only people out there, so I flounce over to the plant pot like I'm about to commit a heinous criminal act, before cautiously turning it over in search of our precious quarry.

'Come on, Al Capone,' Lamont shouts over. 'Get on with it.'

Ahab had sealed the envelope in a plastic sandwich zip bag, to protect it from the elements. Unless these letters were actually being dropped off by Quint all along, of course. Either way, the information was finding its way to us in virtually pristine condition.

Handing Lamont the letter, I sit back and eagerly await its reading. He has his back to a short row of bushes, two feet behind which is the white picket fence.

Full disclosure time.

After a day chasing silver on the Ribble, I'd caught a nice salmon and Lamont had three between two beats. This was some years ago, probably around 2008, and, anxious to share the news of an unbelievable day, we went to the Bay Horse to bask in the glory. Sure enough, a few of our pals were in, all of whom had been fishing without the sort of luck we'd enjoyed: perfect gloating conditions. With six of us sitting around a table in this very garden where Ahab's final clue would be placed, Lamont proceeded to tell us in fine detail – and I do mean the finest detail imaginable – about each catch, right down to explaining the cunning importance of how he angles his body while casting. The only thing missing was a prop, so in lieu of a fat cigar, he rolled himself a joint. Nobody else among us cared, they were very much cool with it, but everybody had shit to do or was driving home, including me, so all declined a drag when offered. Meanwhile, Lamont puffed and talked, puffed and talked, until eventually the colour began to drain from his face and he was forced to announce that he needed to lie down. Thus, he slunk behind the bushes and propped himself up against the white picket fence.

Leaving him to it, we continued chatting with only the occasional glance in his direction. Then, maybe twenty minutes later, I offered to get him a Coke and a banana, but still almost pallid, he sheepishly admitted, 'I have to go now. Something has happened downtown. I think I've shat myself.'

Talk about a good day gone bad! A perfect outing fucked, drawn and quartered, to the point where it can't be un-fucked. Luckily, one of the other lads had an open flatbed truck, and after chucking Lamont's gear in the back and walking him to the rear, he gingerly laid our ailing hero down to rest and recover while he drove him home. Barely able to contain ourselves, we waved the wasted shat man goodbye; the last shot of him being a fist rising defiantly from the floor of the truck as it turned on to the A59.

Lamont did not play out again that season, and the incident passed into folklore. The white picket fence became a totem for unreasonable behaviour, an iconic image of a postcard dream; clean-living sobriety blasted by a gloating idiot with a home-baked brown loaf that's fallen out the oven way too early, due to an involuntary miscommunication between baker and brain. Brain said go, baker said no.

So, it is only fitting that with the fabled white picket fence directly behind him, Lamont opens Ahab's final letter and begins to read aloud.

Aloha Pioneers,
I only wish I'd been there to see it all unfold myself. . .

'The cheeky bastard,' Lamont looks up from the page, glaring. 'I bet even Plato and Aristotle shat themselves at least once.'

This is just a bump in the road, however, and he does continue to read. For my part, I have already lined up all three notables standing shoulder to shoulder: Plato, Aristotle and Lamont.

What an inspiring image.

. . .Naturally, we had to start where our friendship began, with me up to my knees in mud at the bottom of Osbaldeston Hall beat. Sometimes, hell won't leave you alone. Over the years, this spot had been my own little secret – a productive, private secret – but then you boys discovered it and wouldn't leave well alone. You even had a bench erected, complete with a brass plaque that read: 'Ring in sick!' Magic circle rules: never reveal how the trick's done. Too many hard yards on this river, but you helped me that day. I had heard about you both, one a workshy salmon addict, the other a hair-trigger lunatic. There were elements of your characters that reminded me of myself. . .

'He thinks he's Willy fucking Wonka handing over the keys to the chocolate factory,' Lamont breaks off again, his face dripping with incredulity. 'And what's this about a "hair-trigger lunatic," the dick.'

Impatient to hear more, I gesture for him to get on with it.

That night, I decided you two should get my diary, 50 Miles of Lies. You seemed to have the right energy, faith and devotion. In this pool, I got properly emptied. I couldn't stop it – it just kept on going, nothing to be done. I was on the fly and in a total daydream, the river had been quiet all day. The line had just ended its swing when I got a really violent take. This was 5 hours after the tide, so it could have just arrived. Lifting into it, I fully expected a run, but this thing just went and went and went. With the banks too steep to get out and give chase, I tried to get out but just could not manage it, so I shuffled down under the bank in a vain attempt to keep up with it. Fly line out, and now about 80 yards of braid backing – gone, all the way to my knot. Seconds after that, the hook pulled. Never even saw it. Man, what a rush!

50 yards downstream from your bench, at the top of the bank, you will find a decaying log. Roll the log away and dig down about 2ft. When you open the metal tin, there is one more letter and two packages. One of these is my diary, the other is a phone of sorts.

I lived the things I built,
Ahab

Hurriedly and excitedly, we neck our drinks and head to my car, Lamont hugging me all the way to the motor. Travelling a long way from normal, we select Cloak & Dagger by Tommy McCook and the Upsetters; the bassline fits perfectly as we glide down the back roads and into the valley we love. Over the crest of the hill, the river opens out in front of us while we chat glorious possibilities and beautiful nonsense, giddy in a semi-childlike state that feels nothing short of liberating.

We park up, and Lamont gets a shovel from the boot. Walking the three quarters of a mile down to the bottom of the beat, we both agree that it's been too long since we last fished here; by my reckoning, at least four years. To most people, the bottom of the beat is the fence line that borders the woods down the bank and into the river, but we know that the actual boundary is about one hundred metres deeper into the trees.

Hopping over the stile and entering the woods, we see our bench and the young tree we planted for Ahab. Lamont is not hanging about or standing on ceremony, he's off pacing down the top of the bank, counting out his steps like a pirate on a treasure hunt. The river looks very inviting, and I make a mental note to be in this spot from late February before turning my attention back to Tomb Raider.

'This must be it,' he shouts down, from atop a decaying log.

Making my way over to him, I can see that the log is quite large. We each place a foot and start rocking it back and forth until it can be rolled back to reveal a rectangle of compacted disturbed earth. Without a word, Lamont throws me the shovel and I nervously start to dig. Whilst I labour, he reminds me again of the springer he caught here by devoutly recalling the why, where and when. The saying goes, 'If you're going to dig a grave then you had better dig two,' and as Lamont finishes off his recap with the deliberately inflammatory verdict, 'A keen piece of angling that, unlikely to be repeated,' I think I'd like to fully test the one grave theory, but before I can finish imagining myself cracking him squarely across the back of his head and burying him in the hole I'm digging, just like in the movies, I hit something hard and metallic. This stops us both in our tracks momentarily, before I quickly clear off the top soil and use the blade to go around the edges of what turns out to be a green metal box with dimensions of around 2x1.5ft. Each grabbing a handle, we lift the box from its resting place and carry it up to our bench, where I do a full three-sixty just to make sure we are completely alone, determined that whatever is inside is ours and ours alone.

Shoulder to shoulder and almost fluorescent with anticipation, we each flick a latch and open the lid at the exact moment that a huge gust of wind blows straight through the woods.

'Terrence,' Lamont whispers, as we both grimace.

The first thing we see is another plastic bag containing an envelope, under which is an A4-sized cloth sack wrapped and bound by two pieces of string. Lifting the sack out, it's obvious that this is the diary, and beneath it is another, larger object packaged the same way. We place the two parcels on the ground next to the now empty box, and then, using the pocket lock knife my dad bought me when I was eleven, I cut through the strings that bind the cloth sacks.

'Which first?' Lamont asks.

'The book,' I answer emphatically. 'Got to be the book.'

Lamont nods his assent, and I slowly and carefully unwrap the smaller of the two items. Folding back the cloth to see the book, it doesn't disappoint; leather-bound, hard-backed and thick as an encyclopaedia. Ahab had branded the title into the cover, and inside the pages are a mixture of drawings, diagrams, maps and text, utilising pencil, ink and paint to demonstrate feather, fly and spinner designs. Every page is brimming with information and memories, and I know instantly that this is the most important book I have ever had the good fortune to open, its contents so personal and so very close to home.

'This is unreal,' I say, closing the book so I can properly savour it later.

'You big, beautiful, crazy bastard,' Lamont yells into the air, laughing in near disbelief.

Returning the book to its cloth wrapping, we turn our attention to the second parcel. I unwrap it, and we both take a step back and gasp what we find.

It's a Ouija board.

Perspective is a fantastic thing.

'That's brilliant!' Lamont explains.

'What the fuck?' I wonder aloud.

'He did say a phone of sorts,' Lamont points out.

Indeed, he did. A phone of sorts. Until now, I hadn't given that part of the letter a second thought.

'Malkin Tower is just over that hill in Blacko,' I say in a low voice, my gaze fixed on the ever-imposing sight of Pendle Hill. 'In 1612, they tried ten people on trumped-up witchcraft charges, marching them through the Trough to Lancaster and the gallows. On the coerced testimony of a nine-year-old girl, they hanged nine of them, and now here we are, over four hundred years later, digging up a Ouija board in order to contact the dead. All we need is a black dog to appear and suckle at your teat – all the colours of darkness.' Pausing to let all this sink in, I see that Lamont has his arms aloft, holding up Ahab's Ouija board as if receiving a mystical blessing from Pendle. 'You're right,' I laugh, 'it is brilliant. Pure genius.'

My mind is conjuring images of Lamont and I conducting a midnight seance under a pink paschal moon and the magical gaze of Pendle Hill. It wouldn't be the first time we had dabbled in the occult in the name of catching salmon.

Opening the letter, I assume responsibility for reading in front of the class this time.

Congratulations!

You did it. Thanks for indulging me. Take a look at this place, what more could you need? Our home water, our home. The river was my everything, my passion and inspiration.

Make sure you ignore the window dressing and concentrate on the basics. Slow and simple.

If you ever need me for some fine-tuning, just use the board.

Live Deliberately,
Ahab

After a short discussion, we decide to rebury the empty metal box, so the hole is refilled and the log rolled back over. 'Never look a gift horse in the teeth,' is Lamont's reasoning, as we consider its potential as a place to stash whiskey, tackle and contraband. We then silently gather our new treasures, climb the stile and head off up the field.

'Nobody is going to believe this,' Lamont puffs out his cheeks, as he breaks the silence by stating the obvious. 'Fifty Miles of Lies! Let me look after the book, Boo, and I will let you have it when I've finished reading it.'

Like a prospector at a gold strike, he puts his claim in early, his tone of voice straight out of Westminster as it attempts to suggest that he has my best interests at heart.

Another warm gust of wind clears the trees and seems to briefly nudge us apart.

Ahab must be chuckling.

9
Cable Ties and Duct Tape

It's 5:30am, and as I stand in my rented kitchen wearing nothing but a pair of boxer shorts, I stare thoughtfully at the sand ebbing slowly down the egg timer. Watching these minute grains slide helplessly and inevitably into the abyss triggers the daily episode of middle-age dilemmas that flashes through my mind, sending an unpleasant current of nervous vibration through my whole being. My eighty-seven-year-old mother's health is a leading subject of concern, along with the more banal money-related issues. Am I nearly up to my overdraft limit? is just one of many such strobe thoughts. Is the gas bill paid? Will I have enough money to buy the fuel to drive us all back home to Clitheroe? Have I got some work next week when I'm home? Should I get a proper job? Is the man who is on his way to pick me up to go bass fishing actually planning to kill me?

The egg timer only amplifies the point about remaining life and time on a slowly dissolving planet earth; the gloating egg timer and I are big old pals. I make a deliberate effort to shake myself out of it, count my many blessings and keep jamming as I repeat the mantra.

It will be alright, I tell myself. It will be alright. It will be OK.

Upstairs, my sleeping family are all blissfully unaware of the concerns that I silently grapple with. They are simply enjoying a cottage holiday in St David's, Britain's smallest city, a beautiful spot in the Welsh coastal county of Pembrokeshire. The great Italian film director Federico Fellini would have shot this scene in black and white, utilising a flowing stream-of-consciousness style, accompanied by a soundtrack comprising a loud ticking clock, and with interspersing split-screen cutaway images featuring my well-worn, wrinkled face, the cocky egg timer, a set of cable ties and a roll of duct tape.

My soon-to-be companion, the potentially murderous Matt Spence, is en route from Bristol and will be at my front door by half-seven. No doubt, his demented tackle bag will contain such essential items as surgical gloves, pliers, a lump hammer, twenty metres of black polythene and a cheeky little bottle of chloroform. We 'met' online – swipe left! – and I tentatively got to know him over a period of six years or so of following each other on Instagram, during which time we slowly cultivated a friendly rapport. His online persona seemed reassuringly normal, with no red flags that I could tally. For example, if his feed included the phrases: 'Taking names and kicking ass,' 'Bitchin', or 'Off the hook,' red flag. Mosh pit at a Korn gig? Red flag. Crumpling a can of beer against his head? Red flag. Starching his Klansman suit? Red flag. Referring to people as 'chief' or 'boss?' Red flag. Describing food as 'pan-fried?' (Oh, did you have the waiter-served steak, too!) Red flag.

This Matt Spence's online persona makes him appear to be some kind of wonderful, a veritable Peter Perfect, which naturally inflames my growing suspicions. He claims to like cricket and fishing (honey trap!), his potentially pretend family look happy when photographed with him and his very possibly made-up friends all allegedly think he's a fun guy.

Apparently, he's never kidnapped or eaten anybody, the catfishing cunt.

When I posted on Instagram that I'd booked a week's family holiday in St David's for early August, and that I was keen to give bass fishing a spin, Matt offered to meet up and show me the ropes. Of course, such an anomalous level of kindness brought out my natural scepticism, but I accepted his offer safe in the belief that he'd probably jib out at the last minute. However, true to his word, arrangements were made, and since I was the one who requested this song, the least I can do is dance.

With the ETA fast approaching, I have made damn sure that I'm ready for this psycho, right down to the long pants chosen to conceal a Stanley knife stuffed into my sock; no fucker is tie-wrapping me on a fishing trip! Obviously, I took the Stanley knife advice from Lamont, who was highly alarmed upon hearing that I was planning to meet a total stranger. Lamont is the type of guy who abruptly informs people that he has enough friends. He is devoutly anti-new people, hence his final words on the matter being as follows:

'Make sure you do not lead. Stay behind him at all times. This fucker could be a pusher, planning to shove you off a cliff and pretend you had a miscalculated slip. That's his modus operandi, believe me. Think about it, it's the perfect cover. Phase two then kicks in, consoling your wife and family. With you out of the picture, the crazy, twisted bastard will have carte blanche, so you'd better keep a blade in your sock, or else you'll end up being just another photograph on the wall of his private murder cave.'

Peeping through the blinds to glance anxiously down the street, I see Matt the Ripper cautiously curb-crawling towards my temporary residence. Armed with only a beaming smile, he's all sunshine and light as he pulls up to park and I step outside to greet him, and then quick as a flash, he's out of the car and shaking hands. When he opens the boot for me to dump my gear, I'm able to take a swift inventory of its contents: No duct tape? Check. No tie wraps? Check. No lump hammer? Check.

Weapons-based fears allayed, I look into his eyes Larry David-style and offer another strong handshake, having concluded that suspected maniac Matt is not a pusher after all. So, after firing in my slightly inappropriate gear, I nip back into the house to grab my phone (i.e., to ditch the Stanley).

We make easy conversation on the drive down to Whitesands beach as, elated that I'm going to live, I start to relax. Non-threatening Matt has made me a wading stick and brought along a rod, reel and a small box of lures for me to use. My freshwater salmon spinning gear is nearly right for the job, but not quite, and 'not quite' is a recipe for disaster; the elements will devour it and spit it out.

Be warned: measure twice, cut once.

Arriving at the beachfront car park, Fellini's black-and-white monochrome is replaced by an optimistic complexion of vibrant, flamboyant sun-induced colours in the vein of Paolo Sorrentino's film Hand of God. Everything is radiant, golden and glistening, including our outlook, as Matt and I quickly get into our waders and tackle up. He gently explains the nuances of his gear compared to mine, receiving no argument from me after suggesting it would be for the best if I left mine in the car. He is rakish, tall, slim and healthily tanned, and we walk and talk as we make our way towards a large rocky outcrop known as St David's Head. Our aim is to climb down to a cove on the other side and fish the surf on a rising tide; the geography of this horseshoe-shaped cove means that high tide will cover the beach and leave us on a somewhat sticky wicket regarding an exit strategy, with steep cliffs to the rear cutting us off. Alex

Honnold of Free Solo fame I am not; I'd feel uncomfortable on top of his camper van, never mind the 3,000ft granite of El Capitan (no Helicopters, not today). The way in looks mundane enough, but is actually like climbing down an ancient serrated cheese grater; one wrong move, and a broken bone would be the least of your worries. My comfort zone is so far behind me, it's on a plane drinking an emotionally strong Bloody Mary without me, but I've at least remembered to follow Lamont's sage advice and allowed billy goat Matt to lead. He picks a slow, careful route down to the shore, and then confidently calls out as he energetically casts into the oncoming breaking waves, 'I reckon we've got half an hour.'

The water is a brilliant turquoise. The spray from the breaking waves' white foam splashes playfully at my face (alive!), the breeze is on my face (alive!) and the waves are pressing against my chest (alive!), and as I feel the rod bend and load with the weight of my six-inch-long surface lure, letting fly is liberating. Matt has advised me to give this lure plenty of tip action on a slow retrieve – 'walking the dog' was how he eloquently framed it – and I find this whole experience profoundly wild, real and refreshing, fully understanding how it could become addictive. It has instantly mainlined straight into my psyche, containing all the elements of chasing salmon that I enjoy, pimped in neon and dipped in exhilarating danger, as Matt and I work the beach shore typewriter style, shuffling away from and then back to our designated exit spot on the rocks. Neither of us has a pull in the thirty minutes we spend trying, so Matt suggests making our way over to the point on the Whitesands side of St David's Head.

As we approach the point, Matt starts descending down a seemingly ridiculous craggy, ankle-snapping outcrop of nasty human cheese grater, before looking back over his left shoulder just in time to see me refusing like a show-jumping horse at a five-pole fence.

'I can see the fear in your eyes,' he says, smiling. 'Don't worry, we'll find another way down.'

Fear in my eyes? I think. How perceptive! But what about the fear in my ears, nose, feet, fingers and the rest of my freaked-out anatomy?

After gingerly clamouring around to the point, we fish for another hour before heading back to the beach café for a coffee, jam doughnuts and a rethink. Each cast has felt like it was going to be successful, filling me with the wonder of our wild surroundings in a way that was deeply satisfying.

This bug could bite deep.

Deciding to try a spot on the costal path between Caerfai and St Nons, we talk tackle as we weave along a slim, sandy clifftop path. Matt has lent me his Van Staal reel for the occasion, and wow, what an impressive piece of kit. Tightly engineered and salt-waterproof, it's small, light and smoother than gravy, a joy to fish with.

Measure twice, cut once.

Not being convinced of our ability to gain access down these savagely dramatic vertical walls, I happily trot on behind Matt, making more easy conversation and all the while surveying our surroundings. The waves are crashing, the gulls are calling and the soulless, plunging grey cliffs remain ever ready and ignorant. What gravity and rock can forgive, the apathy of a patient sea makes ready to finish. Forbidding is an apt description.

As with all things, there is a matter of degree and perspective to consider, and bass fishing is no different. Some folk kick through the gears quicker than others, many prefer to stick rather than twist, but there are always a few dependant explorers that will push on into the void. Matt outlines a few of these inner bass tribes: the straying wetsuit anglers, who are happy to swim to their favourite inaccessible coastal marks; the zodiac boat anglers, who patrol the crags and coves; and the sea kayak user, hooked up to GPS and radar; all of whom fish with passion and a burning ambition to fill the void and sail ever closer to the edge.

Reaching a sexy-looking spot on the sandy cliff path, Matt searches for an easy route down to the water. Looking over the edge, we see a slab rock ledge approximately thirty feet below us; this ledge looks quite wide, offering a vantage point from which we can fish into a lovely deep azure cove. As Matt navigates his way through the rock that zigzags down the cliff, standing on top of the ridge I can see he has made it with minimal fuss and is now casting into the cove. Time for a few photographs as I compose myself ahead of my own descent, and then I furtively follow the contours of the rock with my left hand while keeping my borrowed rod lofted high in the air with my right; my feet are prodding and probing to get the right amount of purchase on each step until at last I arrive alongside Matt.

'Glad to see you're safe and sound,' he smiles.

'Cheers,' I say, feeling a rolling wave of relief wash over me.

No sooner has the word left my lips than Matt's rod has bent in response to a hit on his lure. He turns to me while playing the fish, grinning as he volleys me with the follow-up line, 'I was only worried about my rod.'

Two hours later, the sun is baking us and nothing has been caught beyond a small pollock. Matt says he wouldn't normally fish in these bright midday conditions, but he made an exception in honour of my visit. I'm truly grateful that he did, as today's sliding grain of sand has shown me something borderline exceptional. Sometimes, it pays to take a chance on a stranger, and I come away hoping that this brief encounter will not be our last.

Who knows, I may even introduce him to Lamont.

10
Croutons in the soup

With my better judgement against a brick wall and with a blade to its throat - I have decided to let Lamont write a chapter. It was either this or a blood sacrifice.

Lamont's Chapter

For the Dadaists and Bill S Burroughs.

Analogue - the story of us now and where we are

suited pest brogue trader failing system glory to the critic the trend setter copy to file obituaries already written plastic journalist editors creep bottom line causes blame accountants leaders idiots egos simplistic solutions knee jerk reactions assignations already assigned kindness a weakness tolerance a hindrance ratings opinions clouded judgement bias ineptitude marathons games inference daydream pillow people speechless cherub portraits mask monstrous intentions tried daily tested flowers wilted innocence victims electorate anaesthetised by fear crushed by anxiety pushed forced miles laugh like drains local tongues wag grabbing lips of the clicking clucking ruling classes gene faced weasels limited intersect disappear trace flowering gain push away to lost positions unreal facts unseen

facts lost facts data spree blast star erroneous loss ignorant
strangling asphyxiate the mind delay expression of need let light
lust baby garble abstract hurt pain of failure acclaimed spoken
vanity pulse storm of time argues the cracks broken memories
of the blistered bones hairs nails and tongue snapped by staring
souls deeply explicit time greed deed relinquished phase wonder
which way blankly announce smiling spirit hope gathers pace
love linked to promise steering tide of dreams sleep across the
solar sun tall haze grass quiver branch bowed kill the distance
meticulous lover tapered lifted owl vase desk shiver pile believe
conquer climb aboard hindered future chalk adolescent seekers
lava flow formaldehyde bloated advertiser praise Terrence

bills potholes and Sunday league football chimneys long
gone fazed returns and human race horses cling on climb on
board spend credit spend debt feed travel apply taken out
money robot life commit how's your cubicle cold call accident
emergency have you been injured in a crash deadline geography
king united kingdom do me a favour religion are you sure
cow and sheep places people breaking trying explain yourself
defecate appraisal positive well done re-enforcements spike
gloss luster light mountain protein howls hear us trying feel us
crying tap talk text speak sex chat and all that internet update
upload refresh update upgrade subscribe sister brother join
in miss out hit out lash out never meet update subscribe like
button protection sanity analogue slow vice head hangover fruit
wake sunshine feel freedom like think of me scab grass wanker
manager boss friend medieval games retro vintage golf dick
cry hemisphere never champagne the fire carbon data prince
shithouse hostile breeder antidote smile on shine on crack on
clap eyes sing wave goodbye blessed dreams memo gazette
consider legal action preserve and protect rum come save us
creatures spirit charity always exemption silver byzantine

zoomorphic permit pelvic thrusters creatures register the
failings negotiate slates feeder blue travel in style clay memories
birds roost phone bidders pin head dealer broke his mirror

hobby lobby watch maker violin pieces united thingdom
anguish stand in line who the fuck would buy rubber trousers
bland on the wall nostalgia silk screen blondie fake tan fake
man true fake flake who am I now oriental mystery clock
whiskey machine colour field handshake forger popular licks
twisted fistula fingers equine tickler craven joints teenage
bullets dirge done better dog dirt dragon established the fact
dispersal blast shards of colour view the decency flag pride
vanity crooked feathers improvised pastels curves gilded guides
jade hunted ashamed haunted vice glass queen map of the fallen
stars magic spells latent talent broad brush apologise its been a
long time coming she's been a long time waiting face the sun
feel the warmth of her gaze love kindness affection no holding
back say what you mean cry out joyful struggle frosted glass
light through the leafs cold love perception collecting thoughts
reinvent reality stop talking you tit zeitgeist following the
like poach the water confirmation rare evolution city limits
education conventionalised a gift given badly not gladly gothic
pulse underground fangs outstretched hops forum vendor truth
asphyxiated bee expenses

one hundred thousand sure is gratifying hide behind the
sunglasses farming squall to grey bloated greed freaks never
trust a man with a pin striped shirt and plain white collar
globally glib festering sores look carefully open your eyes see
transform unlock open not waste art objection reached broken
back bent double split spirits crafted doubts flawed business
leap of faith rested votes languished on shit often bought and
sold ensure poverty local treatment proposed wing explore
signs buried balance insurance clapping search for hope

dance bigger screaming contorted rutting megalomaniacs wheelhouse winter past carbon river plastic planet political pollution spawned ground an artist in search of a medium aortic asshole made me laugh rough with the smothered park bench philosopher belching price cost of charm winking eye bobbing runner weave a stray human copy holds the key exotic climes aggressive chatter louder spent time lost never found countdown mammoth decades still secrets left beating drum baseline hum perfect time savoured shadowed pulse of manumission

Rhythmically admire satsuma sadistic vibrations distance world ripped on speed scorched destroyed by the anarchy pie gliding warmth gentle stream image displayed cramped mind fluid buildings crowing traders grasp unchallenged rewarded results subjective status elevated token trinkets hear the hum of change plastic mountains of greed applied mathematics compound fractions summer spent thrive recent people humans people humans always everyone estimates ignored hear it swimming enveloped senses scenes scenically challenged ribs ingots stoic mothers beautiful wives contrast focus sapping toil demanding crimson themes modern struggles remember what you've seen painting anguish serialised repeated practised colonised repeated cruelty joy celebrated by the soaked lights in town focus on beauty highlight golden moments embrace gestures clearance surface revolver drawn shot fired ghost unsure photographs green parrot rabbits red cap cotton wool breeze past hellos simple premium gilt haze adolescent vanity mushroom discourse cords plucked courage a decoration eggs cracked plotted jacket creeps birth growth acceptance death beckoned age

distracted soft of touch spare beams blinking exhausted night jostling emotions trigger primeval reactions vinyl smiles winter faces arctic dynasty prolific intended anecdotal humour incoherent dominance pioneer manuscript direction unknown closer thieves brown blue green eyes movement makes abstract replica free world associated mess tent press print doubters transcend boiled lemon pudding frankly attempted cold meat cookery domesticated animals trained chimps hoop jumping plate spinning junkies reactive knee jerker's lip service receivers white beards ice creamed lip smacker sun bleached cynic casting recipe groper hope dasher toothy smile spouted shouter pickled questions one thousand moments backward glances true to form dystopia estates jumper painted knees found skipping scars cook book nightmare no I don't know where you bought those pine nuts from wasps against the window mate originals reproduced break beat rhythms thin man gaunt taught face exposed teeth raise a smile explode a laugh cling together fancy emotions gymnastic judgements religiously toxic come cloud gleefully ejaculated

sculpted profile sad sack dad purpose unknown leisures columns chapter squawking gladness merchant olive satellite crusher flipper fluorescing skin dietary concerns flapping youth tone balance novelty lighting straight post communication outlet deep sky lost causes gliding bird fearful excuses made from rust digital bullets step free sweet treat ridged loop memory basket carry water you can sort the rich fields raped planet separate summer days associated fringe haze kneeling hound catapult practice in the glass factory do it baby laugh nice an easy drink the juice that's poured or not write your own story jump maximum orange world kitchen leans smile pepper spray riots on the tree branch slide rooftop hillside born in the sky falling health mounted trophy ceramic flagship emulsion of illusion catastrophe agenda power corruption and show ponies learnt behaviour automatic ephemeral story jumped up rich fossils low on poise elegance retaliation embossed tosser vanity square three hundred and sixty degrees of shite roar with laughter hope she gets it corner man eyes wide watching the street fidgeting waiting for the pressure drop run landlord dodge the bullet duck the blade but don't step stand still magic revolution situation mezzanine mournful for a bright future contrast song repeat the process balcony view choked ocean waves heat rises hope floats evaporates predator mountain slopes passionate dancer wrestler proceeding glassy eyes of the venomous hate puppets schooled biblically publicly highlight concede non story again repeat the eternal circle ideas crushed by the information wave driving expression confession trumpet and house piano joy through endangerment sunshine dopamine

velvet rope burn gratitude bleached teeth media pricks scribe a fine line tell adventure hair smile promotion art program registration stool owl slide scream velvet raft probably understood hear visits anyway knew better watched back change don't change see for yourself aim true love is the detail clearance clutter second chance meet solution discouraged doe eyed economics unbuttoning a shirt probation war minister designated bastard nightclub gesture seamless playback dropped friendships colourful characters and fun sponges avoid those fuckers if you can knowledge kitchen seize leaving desperation erupts everywhere flow through your day dream blue Buddha pockets grotesque acidic gestures sphincter faced cyclists proud highways climbing solo deadly advice always think twice instead delivering giant remote illustrated germs thankful research yoga mat twat secrets of five a side football influencing developmental schemes yellow slate state park party prone puzzle ape evacuation melt your ears off

bondage critically acclaimed cunt kissed neck-bone shown marvellous operate yourself ornate dialogue function steelers time grabbers cold callers salesman disturbance green red hip snake prime love stricken flame dancers vanity thought stream enable the flow reach savoury style glass opaque watering riddle catcher in the baluster handle foremost move on grain growth spread dreams camouflage feather eater fatal vitamins jabber invoices for guilty pushers time thieves vicariously crackdown integrity allowed hollow gestures fabric system kicked flogging merchandise sales spoof weasel solo salsa parade your wears cling to fame observe referencing hotel desk clerk arrived lobby to lean on learn on spread manipulate deviate the flight path customs election impact on stock growth rate domesticate hair gel rather travel trending equity measured level water drop flow rate of thoughts creative long playing record groove sound noise leap waterfall foam against faces struggle for life deceptions reproduce instinct not denied or declined airborne thrust against the negative flow tapered legs cross-member beech tail wag eyes closed scale indented chimney scuttle amplified oil barons

augmented scent scene transcendently chopped vetiver grass lands dance hall smile crude funniest thing I've seen all year complete herring patterns before the eyes concussion by goodwill anecdotes chess set glasses opening your mouth love insulted instead of insulated crack dwindle of structure brighter always brighter as the sun rises I smell the whiff of trouble pandemic transition rates consume destroy opposed against versus go with me antagonise the planet in search of profit bristle what was old is new again what's known is forgotten learn to remember two thousand light years form home future days still nights light reflected and refracted property possessions feelings striding arrogance cosmetically wired mountain juice blister pack income stream thought it was free patriotism refuge tree-tops water flowing wind blowing update subscribe update subscribe update subscribe rental log bug do it to me those things like before sparkling polythene lemon jacket moon tonight real or fixture sideways glances stack smiling seeing for miles pervasion theory sixty six hours in a blown out chair screaming in the corridor chest complaints exit nervous legs shaking knee tops chemical emeralds general subsection killer gorilla sliding uphill to death purple blue wine gums battery blindfolded blood bath climate shadow across the old hit the north pushing water uphill job seeker allowance thanks for that gainful employment middle top bottom twenty cans clinging on anyones guess fuck the night

Forensically yours quite moonless donkey watercolours corresponding come closer now slow and deep Jupiter rainbow over the big seas of dreams blind from hope nibble the branch shared un-subscribe from the opiates of doom scroll life of garden herbs sold back to lovers stooping birds caving spring time miserable scurrying activities of self importance self reproach spit and saw dust of ambition snow deep cold plunging temporary temporal quantity listlessness hush surfeit intubation murmured complaint ironic bended broken inhale it all leaping ladybird pay your rates ignorantly night manager love lusting surrogate father keen to impress backward leaps of intellect full of horse feathers eager to fail in a dismal story ark sixties children playing out hunting for video fun adults hunting for youth lost in a sixty hour week while fingers wag on bookies corner young soul rebels transform hubris into old sold rebels basic succinct squinting at the sun ducking the slaughter home improved bought and sold debt of the past at the cost of the future bananas Buddhas account numbers free trials and call centres welcome to the distraction and you are the driver of that there is no doubt hallucinated by you the narrator check the records do as you are told consume and comment but none deviation or devotion months years days erode to joy countries count the cost borrow admire the Lancashire Lama farmers optimism

Temperance temper dance reliably informed heinously issued warnings love thrust effectually grey rain waring with each drop laughingly drowning grinning ear to ear like an Accrington brick bustling social clubs brimming with toads glad of company shimmering drunken outlooks innocent hostile free speed kills but at times its a fucking necessity of epic proportions wizards spin in Parliament ailment elected from their towers of smiles promising as they tread with grace to reach for power elaborate strategies tragedies built from stealth fearless lies gleaming match winning smiles champion versions of themselves north south east and west plastic complexions featureless willing to lead you honour the corporation who gave you a hand held billboard glowing with promises new and improved bespoke marketing snooze and lose ignore the cost singularity prosperity circles circumference spanned repetition reproached add liberally the punctuated bliss New York state of mind twist erection nature reserved preserved wasted light flowing fields growing the answers are in the soil growth sustainable by way of a lack of greed sunshine creeping wreck folds never reveal the trade tricks gate keepers holding our keys shrouded in education until intellect is tested defined by privilege already refreshed hob goblins bursting balloons swimming in expenses bottled cooked twisted barbarians suited cosmetically sealed protected by their laws pretext the script wired cats sharp pouncing pass the cheese board heartlands grasslands jungle cats tree dweller backstage upstaged worried anxiety state of love and loss gilded cage guided missiles diplomacy tender nurture fittest fastest foolishness cords grinding stunted by glory fluff the lines subscribed to pretences swinging in the backyard

Heatwave voiced ambient colours flowering bushes out of it outlook inward glances vibrant smells flavours eager to impress beach life sea seen toes dipped sun kissed drumming drug postcard over and out with the measurement of an inside leg finest reprehension algorithm to joy ode to joy displacement trustful version coerced with a grin primed pimped sleet sheet ice conversation tapped recorded reordered resold get your glad rags on withering heights joyless examples jump abstinence is bliss furtive tendrils of touch senses overwhelmed calender customs listing boundless possibilities futile gesture positive outcomes curious dogs ready for the chase house piano upbeat bass lines escape the hoard all aboard the next new thing clamour for self improvement work the angle agree to disagree talk show sponsors talk radio contrasting opinion pretended outrage moving on swiftly knee jerk fire starters bewilderment universal arrogant triumph bleached teeth snakes opportunity clocks implode options shouted forced turd compacted squeezed through unplugged ears view of beauty obscured murder moans platitudes of aptitude air tight seamless cloaked in sorrow fighting for joy bubble freedom the goal grief heavy suffocating the weary wondering public feeding on an apathy frenzy fingers age old moonshot

Sweet heart of salted tears reduced to tears weekly thrive breathing but grieving folded speed chaser missing the point time in your pocket features in your mind but forgotten with instruction projected needs greeds of others two thousand year old sky broken stars gifted importunity practising capsizing in the job club beauty across the desk blank smile blank outlook pen pusher with a shimmering outlook sink into the river of the world pulse raiser stare master reticent extension autocracy lapped up kiss his diamond shoes because of you radius and ulna spring loaded for a slap where and when you shout into the breeze of the river empty eyes stained by your past bewildered by your future clap hands stamp feet bleat to the few that care raise the flag to uncertainty to the unknown of not knowing celebrate stamp clap shout stamp clap shout into the wind scream into the mountain commute to the community of erstwhile forgers eclipsed smartly by warmth sunshine on your features radiant skin perfect skin flexed taught and impressive in statue really though another subtle echo from patience worn thin laughing friends robotic behaviour subscribe colour describe destinations tactile inhibitions influencer by a crazed self proclaimers

Your smiling face you've gained some weight cheers for that you cunt get them told in from the cold conceited constituted killers witty pithy misbehaviour warranted surprise seeds and pulses will set you straight white rabbit chicken shit star man blasting the debate with hindsight go get them tiger what you should of said bullshit the morons with endemic accomplishment file under knob-head talking round corners inflated flatulent star fuckers gravity classroom Olympics trip camera jet stream geographic ions looking out of the back of the bus now we lap up banality like its normal subscriber push to the front of the crew health and safety seed breaks open with water and light no regrets one shot at the title stretch the canvas and wet your brushes paint your own picture the way you look tonight dancing girl glow shine forcefully dance joyously laugh wildly red terracotta fired buy the earth blame tame all the same armed to the teeth capitalise energise vocalise solidify modify months time erode purity notifiable advertises pacify tea coffee and other drinks are available ground papilla nineteen zero three crushed bones heightened senses applicate floored by the logic of an unasked question glittering smile match-winning smile big hitter long driver top forehand smile glowing tan untrustworthy snake charmer ladder climber chop them at the knees and don't look back full swing swigging fro the bloody chained cup of history

Down in the canyon sleeping in Martha's vineyard resting on their royalties living off a dream stare into the warm night air stars damaged as they glimmer of hope howling wading bird looping in the humming bird sky sisters clinging sides splitting dappled by sunshine playing the part loading their shopping carts squinting with humour eyes sparkle in July meanwhile across the bay envy gives way to hate jokes unfunny laughing out loud crying out lout lout fingers the air to a digital beat bump bump bump bass head radio worth more than the car you know the type clinically cuntish its no coincidence flight school walking tilted for trouble geared for annoyance glass jar jar manhole mouth a bad combination just add drugs and alcohol cheers ears beep beep beep tech-no beat gos beep beep beep like his plastic face look nicely dance wisely remembrance affectionate but better left behind ugly mistakes seven day heroes forward thinkers ambivalence therapy abstract splats in the high rise flats vertical Pollocks visceral media balcony jumpers gluttony and the lash irate catching bullets in their bum cheeks eight days a week hide and seek from the law enemies sentimental asides sat at night trying to crack the worlds biggest mystery of lost friends angels devil dogs and rizzlas piss were you stand hold the lift

Smug and pliers thats the game of thrones on this estate escape and evade dream big or go home split the atom and disappear its not rocket science stainless steel meat hooks resident rain equals less bother for the cops theres an inducement of reality incidents in a climate in decline saline sanity down the concrete steps into television land furniture occupied by ghosts built by children shipped at low prices by the repressed dress easy but at least it was cheap rejoice reduced to tears rag trade of misery give him a knighthood for stealing pensions cheers for that I hope his boat fucking sinks hit by torpedo of cheap tear stained socks the fat tanned toad ridged dome box cube and sprinkler system raining on the joggers as they pass built from suburbia and back handers good arrows with his hand pinned to the board bicycles on the street global climate strike wildlife conservation obviation station funding feeding fledgling policy of good deeds done community planning eating up the land the reckoning will be inherited highlights sustained edited recored touching feeling reasoning thought processes isolated net loss through petulance modern life acid tested if the field and on the fells infected love affair for a nature lost in a flurry of hurry bio diversity wilding forests trusted up in still life woodlands stopped in time

Face your reflection charted journey cramped travel battery hen tube train stratagem nimble response overcrowded purple heavy threaded seats knees tucked under your neighbours chin hazel eyes hoping for contact next stop natural selection dip your gaze he looks like he wants a chat fuck that read all the posters instead study the map inspect the line close encounters of the train kind rather blasted into space than take another shot of small talk the smallest talk in the history of tiny talk where do you get off where ever you don't where do you get off oh really I get off after look at your phone freckle faced ticket butcher happy in her work collecting bats droppings to make the flowers work embedded with vulgar thoughts freaked out at the weekends uniformed in the week familiar with body odour unfamiliar with success palm oil in the armpits locking up carbon re-watered wet lands double benefits better squeal to the sir concrete baron before the share price dips he's infested with crypto-currency trickle down loose lips sink ships derby construction industry software universe analysis family counting the cost describe the lie spitting mountain surreal overhead shot at the world invisible an application of obscurity a acceptance of love open hearted flowers in the medieval courtyard paradise hillside village snaking climbing streets under a grey society of clouds

Translator has the takeaway arrived lentil and turmeric by numeracy mercy me folklore of legs and knees officially merchandise divine birth right to a pizza wooden chiselled bowl humility in its statue arms outstretched exciting news of the new democracy president elect capacity elected mental ascribed unwise decisions neck ache voter quintessentially institutionally facile dog bark waring the masters jacket letter of complaint on the free world culturally invincible scoring goals in buckets playing the beautiful game agreeable schemers ill fitting suits walking talking battling robots with the real power in the back weather beaten wet faces peer to the wind with patience and impatience in equal measure fish tail parker and bubble coat huddle in the yard expectantly in anticipation of all they hold dear brow beaten and pestered by gleeful optimists keen for the future to arrive surly unruly burning life force elongated tarmac holding whispers of water and reflections of youth sparks in your eyes flame with a passion for simplicity a potion not too poison years sped by like a lullaby as you remember those exact words from your parents wasted on your youth don't wish time away it will pass you in a flash reflection is a destination direction

Hoof prints beached bleached in gold risen from the depths ripples in the sand tide ebbing out bloated swollen sea birds cry out as the stage sets up for another day in reverse sky chastened chained in a natural act of diplomacy landscapes as portraits elated by opportunity forlorn in appearance abstract by design sovereign celebrations national pride turning wind turbine generating hope engineered and planted into a surprised mountainside the little girl looks startled as her red balloon drifts away nine million reasons to paint another the preening princes and the coat tailed paupers bilge filled hedge funders at play egos sweat and saw dust on show case bicep curl erection fortunate sons heirs and graces water wheels revolving confusing critical acclaim riding luck like a racehorse champagne region celebrates euphemisms like snowflakes fall on greedy swine snouts in the trough hollow gestures guilty pleasures rip offs and cover ups behind a coercing smirk one more bid madam avant garde arrogance hit it and quit it

Green lipped muscle car triumphant spitfire tip toed dancer breaking mothers leash lashes out in blinkered rage have you seen Mick the chicken take seven for seven real deal route one zero one California out run through Big Slur thrifty second street music pimp trading punches Internet providers bedroom giants down town pricks cheerful goats outraged lamas no drama lama jovial betrayals pats on the denim coated back Milan in the seventies goaded coffee houses window gazing executives under hand antics woven into free flowing fabric normalisation limbs cut fractured broken systems vagrant alone scared vulnerable trusted murderer hiding in plain sight tragedy awaits under street lights easily arranged watch schemers not the parking meters inanimate objects fisted rebuked movement keys pride rises Rome awakens salt on its lips vertebrae coiled linen sheets waiting comfort surrounded architecture of nature brutalised ideologies skipping down cobbled streets sexualised shed collapse aimed for off stump turkeys at the crease fecklessly wafting flowers of romance pointing up the chimneys examining the turrets preparing deleted tweets underground six feet ground beneath your feet face harp in the key of G

Safely first resin clinging strung out clinching the deal its a race to the top mate not the bottom smugly stated by the coked up plumber charging seven hundred fifty a day play ground tactics old equaliser throbs network sobs water to bone Id like to know where you got the notes from landslip uprooted river-ed out on last card turned original gamble gamstop everyday worldwide wonders Lancashire to Tennessee in an instant clearance of the laboratory revealed dark secrets paint by numbers power by numbers orientation of land lines rolling granite forming drama changing the family name at close range hieroglyphics language left for the milk man he wasn't happy said he wanted cash Monkey cars welcome to the greed pit of the charmless billionaires

Armstrong fan Strong logo mixed message on uncommon ground laundering the monies like Lionel all night long sucker MC's throwing funky bones softly spoken then bended then branded high rise voices shrill in their output fatefully pronounced announced onto speed contracts fulfilled love lost word up man you don't know who I am hero's to villains along campaign trails followed by trials classical string section disciplined orchestrated spent the day flying in the Hadron poetical collider you can turn it on and sleep through your shift room service work force steeped in crude kudos inter-dimensional front libel metaphysics budget coup interesting mistakes alleyways and walk ups spitting into broken bottles magic stars of New York old England oak woodlands turned urban jungles north south east west humdrum similarity sadness labours and dispatch riders glide into the night

Scurry stations toothy smiles gladness gurus fucked by a wellness coach next to badness torn sky ripped memories ecstasy in tiny damp rooms in abstraction ideology morality work shy shiftless bar on the corner bar brawler out for love bursting his lungs to slow down chased by moray eels whistling gentle slaughter such a sweet story imitation game injecting the amputation game ejected from world abducted from self piano notes played tangled into song ruby red robins gossip spying in plain sight Latin names learnt to use when Erithacus rubecula Carl Linnaeus to thank first hand her knowledge of Latin fell on dull ears interview failed panhandler shattered face of the Baltic boxer neon prophecies of the contest promoter lips to the pipe people bent with laughter enjoying their big night hanging onto each other kitty shared drumming beats of winter hail tap down window pains hospital patients longing for home alpine resort splatting arguing paint resistive wildly applied trapped roving nights avalanche emotions skiing off piste drug cure

Pills knocking sleep away unrecognised platitudes exchanged by time and place circumstance buoyed by waste nothing needed or wanted stoned stupor shifting through the gear resurrected with a pay cheque freshened by a shower wheels back on go again avoid hate of the half fullers who's got time for that surrounded my positivity bound by invisible gravity dead weight detective looking at a sewage spill hit it and quit it unknown robots grafting up the escalator bargain hunters with sales in their eyes ambition is a saving more than enough greed for two clock faces shudder as the market drops daisy chain in the shredder clogging up its teeth waves crashing up the cliffs border control birders on the count checking for migration fair and pleasant land defective deflated by its past slavery of the seas stolen people in transported from countries on their knees war torn landscapes and that's just their faces warped by anger congealed by fear running for the boats follow the sun shooting for freedom hoping for safety mighty penmanship folded to the sword of the dictator tightening its grip screaming fleeing conger up the thought of flight flighting for your life flighting for children

Almost nearly always count the chickens in scarlet velvet suits whistling at next door moments of truth plastic contenders bar code efficiency as the window cleaner arrives to have a moan wearing the forecast as a face beyond the thunder dome of the non league stadium roman coliseum to watch the mice fight badger bate gladiators battle for credibility global pay per view cheer for the blood sport of violence ten thousand pundits displayed in bold type at a cost subscribe coming soon rock bottom death match seventeen a pillow fight between bedroom trolls living too late partisan philosophers painting up a storm for the next exhibition

Rich man come down dark continent burning down the corn skiing in the snow clenched fist Northern athletes dance instead of rioting quiet struggle the demons silent never making a sound plotting a negative outcomes lost in a dream of motion as the music plays world suspended floating emotions transferred into the magic of a moment shared experience transcendental casino send offs internal memory evacuation the drug that is not fatal encrypted vigil facing a baton charge fingertips run the edge of the rough tree bark plotting a course for its wisdom of years exuberance of youth diminished extinguished by the terminally weary campfire dampened by a jaded outlook avoid ignore sabotage their narrative lean on the stimulated under gleaming sunlit skies insulated by warmth of feeling southern comforts travel versus static currents flow life force eased within the natural ebb seasons sleepless settled weather cycles dependencies as the game sets in shadows disperse mirrored wanderers classless shadows internal clock shine free listen self thoughts agreed confident strides aggrieved limbs stiff joints untested water cupped wild runs out of grasp here is now and now is the past knock on the door to catch your breath

Teachers shared in the centre of the bridge rain held on the zephyr touches her face once drenched by love ghosts over her shoulders bones to glass unwitnessed unrecognised feelings splintered binary in process convivial clarity cold blooded congeniality waves goodbye erosion office life mimicry winters song of screen time correspondence hopefully expectancy flip the record from sour milk attitudes comedy of chattering teeth search for olives in the garden grapes in the vineyard existence briefly confirmed with a sip of sunshine life toil the land swim in the river run wild in the wood manufactured down the motorways suffocated in the cubicle automated services growth markets expected goals appraisal interviews sickness records measure accountancy recorded future predicted golden messengers convenience assured triumph hurdled visions held on the land stony outcrop walrus face crashing sand storm return to the planet and squall living colour preening at the lions main risk worry and the working week long road to uninstall self protection in the woods head against the window nervous with ideas dreading celebration clasping to the rail

Folded tea towel crumpled jumper momentary silliness brought on by a song teenage dance moves mind colour blind following a crowd towards the sounds gladness ensured floats on silver moist smiles sweet in thoughts polished stones beach front benches pointing out to see hands held half a century life went by so fast at least they had each other sliding through the past blown by circumstance beauty wholly intact complete vision within each others eyes Autumn crystal creeps wild hop spike propagation roots versus rhizomes underneath skittish flock feral attraction lactic acid house going full gas bumper to bumper time assassinates cells vigour relived from duty sixties style apres ski head first your desk slalom into the saloon chased by euro-pop porcelain Monday mornings bugged by the sample pigeon pecking at your head geometric observations regrettable

tenuous threadbare Burgundy suitors waspish in reparation
unlikely in reciprocation globally stunted maniacally inclined
empty space where a face should be petals flowering for the first
time you could have gone show jumping into the canvas on a
painted horse and ridden into the distance too beautiful

Dusty boots in dusty rooms will fly grey surface irregular
squares fissures vertical felled by dogs staring chattering
children scamper herded by mother goose into the trees chasing
along the stream hoots and happy shouts pure joy innocence
living protesting the protesters poster tickets scalpers verbose
in sentiment paradise lost in a tale of one city hillside horizons
double vision celluloid director living in a movie performance
art with consequences ally cats baited claws focused on the fool
blond king timber wolf chained wreck neck search and employ
single frame projector black and white images rolling seeded
speed queen motel foyer voyager trees bent in response almond
smiles bedouin wanderlust glide into view a skyline one of these
days brighter lighter abstract splashes freckles of light yellow
sand reflects euphoria in touch togetherness shared experience
unburdened ivy enveloping the tree trunk separate yet one
parasitic relationship mutual gratification debated puristic in
goal animated dreams played out in two minutes thirty eight
seconds eyes locked in the magic of the moment

How the incline is viewed is paramount wide open spaces
adults child free playground on the empty roundabout broken
glass underfoot litter minded hope a forgotten currency bird
song drowned by traffic too many birds in one tree leaves
exploded scattered global citizens town and country planning
tarmac concrete steel cold in sensation freezing in warmth
right down the line no bikes no ball games joyless space walk
permanent concrete features salt and vinegar yesterdays news
crown jewels united kingdoms clotted cream come down

rooftop remonstrations ball stuck in the gutter propelled heart broken cuts across the land wedding day shouts sneezing groom give her room slicing guest list of unwanted chancers spewing out the dust storm dreaming of the past pulse raised control lost in the haze drunken temper soiled hurt tear felt regret jealousy inflamed by insecurity pride worn heavy pain swallowed weeping by the willows cigarette shaking right handed drizzle lit dreaming of the past

Doorstep stood expectant for entry father denied his face wore his pain my youth stole my judgement familiarity bred contempt conceit stole my head it ended in tears as I felt his final goodbye shadows cast sparkle those eyes gleaming grins movement gave chase ideas locked transparent motives hidden ghetto scenes replicate acceptance speech twenty four seven can do attitudes seeker sensuality airborne fragrances spring steps lifted lightly optimism a vehicle forty nine thousand on the clock driven like a hire car vigorously petulant prejudice extreme gilded splinters gilded fuckers bright faced swollen greed hounds foaming at the dealership under diamond shower street lights baited centres honey coated smilers suited brogue trader tissue thin integrity menial mentality porously teeing off at six celestial bodies take a hit dancing in the living room floating in a fog of joy coupled by song and sound problems dissolved temporarily evaporated hair bounce arms wave bodies revolve sway vigorously in a unity of love

Real around the piazza aromatic convivial poverty piety stretched like a marquee canopy covering the laughing tones stock sunshine smiles generations waspish wise whisperers tanned history lived through rumours sperentia winkles their features red wine at the lips antagonists antagonise salient heroes and valiant villains all pets roam welcoming familiar with the air content with comfortable conditions arched backs for attention grinning for a kindness seductive sounds cheerful chatter has fingers stroke home softly palms ease along backs under chin verbal vulgarity ugly contentment mirrored affection returned music mimics mood casually play playful in spirit reflections of fathers mothers sisters and brothers appropriate renditions gently persuade ensembles celebration embracing tradition or a continuing charade the sun shifts in an illusion legs swing from stone walls fleeting courage of ourselves freedom on the vine

Reservoir of excitement stone built platform cold north east wind penetrates bone teeth grit nostrils flare wincing coffee coated thinly disguised early morning stagger barley sober head throb robs another morning all in a days work dog tired by violence of banality bullseye targets met by squawking passers street wise six feet tall flamingos awkward sliding knees pressurised candy floss gregarious behaviour applauder from balcony tourism inept culture vultures circle on the tow path industrially participant latch key wanderers rum avenger cornish eyes naan bread hair do original upsetter navel gazing bar tenders brassy in style cheap in outlook emptying the slops inert gases in memory of dreams stagnant thoughts loan rovers snapped ankles can you here me captain tom recycled variant heavy eye lids cope jungle joke tour date agent grasping clutching at clouds riding the keel wave wind at their backs

Danger in her eyes youth soul faint heart always safe challenge dining out refusal drop the lid tin hat on foals in the field talking licking their eyebrows nineteen ninety one chrome plated bullshit nostalgia smog practice lives plasticise people fuzzy felt lifestyle gurus blowing tidal in opinions wing loop feathers fluffed plumage plumped acoustic swelled fan assisted phone calls temperature adjusted air conditioning apparent stars carried on cheap blued eyed pillow talk tempters out liar outlined in plan silver hair survivalist aluminium alimony in a can legal fees festered piano notes struck luck diverted for another day tangled underfoot tongue cry concentration of desire feisty determination satisfaction guaranteed siestas of the heart terminal conditions humanity apart looking out the diving bell aorta valve into the unknown pulse swim roam flow followed instinct engage biology beyond your command carousel encounters faded wilting boys and girls skirting a raging mile

Uneaten aliments invisibly unseen velvet apertures in raptures lump hammer ladder ditch at the end of the parade blue sky remorse shotgun hanging on the wall tombstone brain bleed unhinged metaphor needs no introduction as the harmonica story enfolds delighted in mistrust deluded noble theory proved back gate brewers dabblers bar room bombers hard back hoarders invasive sugar charm swindlers with god on their side aspirations fortified in friendship clutched to the chest doorstep philosophies muddled inhibitions glory hunting flourishes involved in the tonic of false rumours spying glass visuals facial wrinkles won vibrantly waiting for the image selected back story clear critic met inspired novelist spat idea pollen in their veins guided by desire insecurity on the reins institutions flamed tolerance stamped all the birds are leaving they just know when its time to go

Dog rolling in a dust filled hall slippers on its feet gelded joints frustrated folk song bitten in verse blues asylum thunder running on empty a pawn in the game wondering oblivion dolly sisters cheer cocaine nights cubical filled eight pairs of feet neat discrete yellow wailing synchronised laughter greeted the fastidious champ fired as a cannon ball exit stage right all aboard the bar tab lets go round again blind expressions pissing in the wind who will win the sprint race fiddle plays the tune of sorrow decide slide rule figure skating perfection commentator cursed with implications racist familiarity dramatic affectations theatre of genes us versus them every word meant forever jerk chicken stashed written law fitness race plank prone plankton hitch hiked county oceans flung opinions dealt quest fallen old tip halo aloft reality marinated in lust all piss and wind cliff face receding foam headed wave crazed glazed glass finish shoreline charted damp footprints single file interview detective rising poisonous tides sombre catastrophic news doom scroll on click on and on

We are but croutons in the soup of life. Namaste - Lamont

11
Easy Rhythms, Random Notes

The sense of anticipation is palpable; we've been waiting for a day like this for quite some time. Summer dragged its heavy heatwave feet while its hands slowly choked the life out of our river for nearly four months, leaving the water a shadow of its former self, to the point where fishing it would have felt like kicking a man while he was down. Autumn finally approached, carried by a dry September, and it soon became undeniably apparent that the Ribble salmon season was in danger of slipping through our fingers, fuelling a growing belief that our season had been stolen from us.

The heatwave had left me wounded. My equilibrium was off.

Finally, October brought the rain. The river got up off the canvas, revived; it felt like a fair fight. Work was cancelled, days off were booked and the river height was never far from our frontal lobes. My phoned pinged with the news that the Ribble was carrying two feet at Grindleton bridge, and that the colour was dropping out. This meant nearly ideal conditions to fish the fly.

Nearly would have to do.

When rare days like this occur, it's of vital importance that you don't share your precious time with some annoying prick. Make sure the foot fits the shoe; friendships are to be curated and cultivated over many years. We're all in the editing suite all the time, and so unfortunately, some relationships will end up on the cutting room floor. Harsh though it may seem, the world keeps turning, and as you slide down the greased pole of time, you realise the character traits that suit your own personality.

Twelve years ago, I moved from Blackburn to Clitheroe. I knew only one person in Clitheroe, and he didn't fish, which meant it was time for me to put my hands in the soil and join the local fishing club, Ribblesdale Angling Association. While fishing the club beat at Low Moor, I was quizzed by a number of suspicious locals, most of whom appeared to have never ventured far over the cattle grid. The most intriguing of these locals were the Holmes brothers, all three of them (Ryan, forty-eight; Karl, fifty; and Marc, fifty-three). I was told by the chairman of the club that it was better for the organisation to have them as members rather than try to deal with them as poachers, and if I had to put labels on their individual qualities, they would be as follows: Ryan is cool and laidback, Karl could happily worry a rat and Marc is stoic and no-nonsense. Whenever they come to mind, I always think of the Three Billy Goats Gruff.

I quickly learnt that the Holmes brothers know everybody in Clitheroe, and that they're on first-name terms with most of the returning salmon, too; they grew up fishing the Ribble, and their relationship with it is an intimate one. Through fishing, we slowly gained one another's trust and a quiet, respectful friendship blossomed, built on the common ground of us all being equally salmon bonkers. Addicts always seek out like-minded souls to ease their own justification template, birds of a feather and all that, and having levelled-up from most of our sedate, care-free, wandering lonely as a cloud, fellow club anglers, we were mutually plugged in and turned on.

After several years of bankside work parties, club events and trips, I began fishing with Marc on a regular basis. We had both become members of Clitheroe Angling Association in search of new water, a fresh challenge and maybe, just maybe, some low-hanging fruit in terms of catches, and so it is that today, 6th October 2022, I pull up on the club car park to find him getting into his spotlessly clean waders, van doors open to reveal an extensive selection of pristine kit: segmented reel bag with tips, spare spools and at least five different lines. Everything is small, compact and, most of all, neat. Marc is spectrum-level neat; he looks like he's been ironed. His flies are all on parade in perfect uniform rows of various patterns in ascending order of hook size; it all makes perfect sense. He is ultra-methodical, taping the joints on his rod every time all the time, an ideal yin to my yang.

My rod is still set up from my last outing; I just wrap the sections together with hair bobbles borrowed from my daughter, to stop them bouncing around in the car. Tape my joints? Oh, who's got the time? All my gear lives in a 1950s canvas post sack, my blended fly boxes are an eclectic mix of assorted sentimental memorial tins left over from fallen comrades; the actual contents of the tins are so traumatised that even I sometimes grimace when opening them. My poor flies look like they need rehab, as though they've been battered in an ugly barroom brawl or recently freed from Mötley Crüe's tour bus; there is zero order, it's Beyond Thunderdome in there. Meanwhile, my wading jacket is rip-ridden, my hat has an ever-expanding hole in it and my waders leak bilaterally.

'I couldn't live like that,' Marc just looks at me and shakes his head. 'You're not well.'

It's 7:45am, and expectations are high. Marc caught a brace of salmon last Sunday, and I managed a 14lbs fish the following day during a quick, lucky hit-it-and-quit-it session while my van was getting new tyres put on. This treasure of a fish had got me off the mark, lifting the mounting pressure of a blank season from my shoulders.

Like I said, the excitement is palpable.

Our first mission is to cross the river and save ourselves a one-and-half-mile walk to where we want to start fishing. The current height is the maximum level for us to get over safely; the water is fairly pushing through, and at the deepest part it's up to my stomach. There's a solid amount of force pressing against us, and for a nanosecond, while we're right out in the open, I wonder if this is such a good idea. This lapse in conviction is short-lived, though, as we plough on and get over and out the other side in a matter of minutes.

Marc thinks our chances will improve as the water drops off, and sure enough it's starting to clear. Winds are over 20mph, so casting will be fun, but the two pools we want to focus on are shielded by high banks on our side and trees on the other, giving us half a chance to get it right. As well as the wind, there is also the challenge of endlessly falling leaves, and as we sit at the head of the pool having a brew, we discuss our respective set-ups. He's chosen a full floater with a slow-sink tip, to which he adds a 15lbs Maxima mono and a dropper ring, and then another 30" of Maxima mono. On the dropper, he puts on a size-12 gold Willie Gunn double; the point is a small Willie Gunn tube with size-10 double.

When I fish with Marc, there are never any headaches. We each always offer the other the option of going through a pool first, and there is a natural rhythm to the sessions; competition is totally redundant. This methodical approach is a million miles away from what I'm used to with Lamont, who insists on covering as much water as possible, often getting through two beats twice in one day. He refers to this approach as 'bare-knuckle fishing.'

I advise Marc that between the wind speed and the river basically being giant bowl of a leaf soup, fishing a dropper may not be the best idea. My set-up is a 13ft rod and full floater, with an intermediate tip. Forgoing my usual dropper, I go for a 19lbs, 6ft fluorocarbon leader to an inch-long Red Francis; the last thing I need are tangles or any additional self-made problems. Then, popping in my headphones, I head two hundred yards upstream to listen to a new playlist while I fish through the Boundary pool, with Pendle Hill looming large as the Fall start their cover of the Beatles' A Day in the Life. The water, the elements, the movement, the view, the anticipation, the music. . .a distorted wet dream.

An hour passes as I slowly fish through this abstract landscape. It must be the season of the witch; recently, I can't look at Pendle without thinking about the falsely accused making their long, sorry march to the gallows along the Trough of Bowland. There is something profoundly mystical about Pendle; it's never the same colour, standing both ominous and beautiful at the same time, a truly captivating sight. Coming to the tail of the pool, I haul myself out, gripping the damp grass bank, music off as I wander back down towards Marc, who has just come out of the Garage pool and is inspecting one of his anal-perfect fly boxes.

We have another brew, and then I go through the Garage pool myself. Nothing shows up, but while casting left hand up is not my favourite thing in the world, I'm pleased to see that I'm slowly improving with practise. Marc goes through Boundary, and now it's time for lunch. He's brought some lovely deli sandwiches, and I've packed a large Roy Porter's pork pie and a decent piece of Proctor's Precocious Cheddar, real rock-n-roll stuff. For dessert, my mum has made us some carrot cake, and as we eat it, my mind drifts to her recent Alzheimer's diagnosis, and the fact that she's eighty-seven now.

Sun rises, sun sets, with life in between.

It's nice to have a slow day with nowhere to be but here. Sometimes, just chatting provides some perspective, and fishing never lets me down, ever. Marc gets away to fish quite a bit, so lunch is full of stories from the rivers Tweed, Derwent and Spey, while I chip in with some local Ribble gossip and a few of my half-cocked theories.

Lunch over, Marc has an announcement.

'I don't play games,' he says. 'Watch me get one out of here now.'

He gets in halfway down Garage and starts to cast. I position myself twenty metres below him, sitting quietly high up on the bank, and after ten minutes he is directly below me and casting to the hot spot, landing just short of the far bank before beginning to pull across the pool. Suddenly, the line moves sharply.

'That's a fish,' he shouts, bending into it as it runs downstream in typical heavy, thump-thump salmon style. 'See, I told you. I don't play games.'

Getting the net, I slowly climb down the bank and into the water below him. He gains line on the fish and tells me that he thinks it's taken the dropper (the same one I recommended he not use); the result is a 7lbs hen fish.

We unhook the fish in the water and get it back on its way pronto; smiles all around as we bask in the glow of a shared experience. It's a rare thing, a salmon on the fly in the Ribble, very much a magic cherry-on-top moment, so we rest the pool again and head off downstream to try our luck; nothing doing, though, as we fish through another four pools before deciding to have the last hour back on the Garage. During our walk back up the field, we laughingly discuss the prospect of being able to do this for another twenty-odd years if we're lucky. Hopefully, life is a marathon rather than a sprint, in which case, maybe it's time I start eating healthy and taking up yoga. Use it or lose it, as they say.

On second thought, I'll stick to my long-planned managed decline. Less effort and more sedate.

Back at the Garage pool, I go through and receive a heart-stopping thug of a tug that unfortunately ends there. Marc tells me to take two steps back and go through again, so, repeating the process, I let my fly swing through again.

Nothing.

Heading for the tail of the pool, I fish it out, cast and step, as Marc gets in the head and starts his run down. The river has dropped around four inches during our session, and the wind had made the lower pools fairly tough to fish, but thanks to the Garage's aforementioned natural shelter, I'm able to sit back on the bank and enjoying some soup while I watch Marc cover the hot spot again. No doubt this time, as his line shoots away with the weight of a fish; this time it charges for Greenland, and Marc is forced to hang on. Slowly, he claims line back and walks the fish back up the pool; one, two, three more thrilling jumps and head shakes, and I'm there ready with the net as he slides in a cracking 12lb-er. Hands are shaken after the fish is released, with broad smiles marking an unreal experience. Luckily, I have brought my decent camera along to better capture the essence of a genuinely rare day.

The sun is setting, and clouds begin to shroud Pendle as we cross back over the Ribble and make our way to our vehicles. Marc always has a couple of cold beers in his van for packing up and reflection; this evening they provide a fitting added zest. He is obviously elated as he meticulously puts all his gear away exactly where it belongs, whereas I sling my torn jacket, leaky waders and bobble-banded rod in the boot. The scene reminds me of Felix and Oscar from Neil Simon's The Odd Couple; Marc would be Jack Lemmon, and of course I'd be Walter Matthau. I'd mention it to Marc, but I'm afraid it would be lost on him; he's more of a River Dance kind of guy. That's fine by me, though. Friendships need to germinate before they truly blossom.

Hopefully, we have at least another twenty years to mature together.

12
EA, Eh?

Having decided to accept joint custody of and equal visitation rights for Ahab's book, and agreeing to only read it when in each other's company, Lamont and I devise a rota of weekends and nights for getting together to go through it. Our plan is simple: digest every facet of information in time to fire into 2023 like meteors, assuming the weather doesn't incinerate us again, of course.

Most of the population have loved the summer of 2022, as paddle boards, dinghies, kayaks and a mutated multicoloured carnival of inflatables adorn our waterways. Our fish counter figures were going through the roof at Waddow Weir, only for us to eventually realise that it's just my son and his mates joyously using the fish pass like the log flume at Alton Towers. Every day, people broil in their hot tubs and throw another tyre on the barbecue – my family contrived to hide my rain stick to prevent me cursing this most blessed summer – whereas for me, if May, June and July were tolerable, and August barely bearable, September is flat-out taking the piss. Hamlet's soliloquy, that's me that is. Full-blown Withnail.

'I have of late – but wherefore I know not – lost all my mirth, forgone all custom of exercises. And indeed, it goes so heavily with my disposition that this goodly frame, the earth, seems to me a sterile promontory.'

No amount of cheese, pies, wine, beer or Test Match Special can lift me from my funk; even the lion's arseholes (sausage rolls) from Stansfield's fail to elevate my mood. What's the point of me if I can't fish? My pilot light is out, as everywhere I go, I am met by burning crimson, wide-eyed, gawking, wild reptilian caricatures all foaming at the mouth, lapping up the sun and hoping it will never end. My body, adapted for around one hundred river visits a year, is now down to a grand total of six, enough to put me in toxic shock. So, bubble burst as I flail around in a desperate attempt at escaping my new reality, I sign up for some work parties with the aim of turning a spiralling negative into some kind of positive by performing some much-needed bankside maintenance in all the hard-to-reach spots.

While cutting back some overhanging branches on our Nappa beat near Gisburn, I have an unexpected encounter; Lamont and I are trimming the overgrown jungle of branches when I realise there is a resting salmon almost under my feet. With the river gasping below summer level, I am wearing wellingtons instead of waders – that's how shallow it is – and after getting Lamont's attention, I put my hand under the fish and gently tickle its belly. The salmon is perfectly silver and in superb condition, but due to the heat it was in a trance, lying doggo (i.e., completely switched off). Stopping work immediately, we slowly depart to another area, leaving the fish to what it was obviously claiming as a safe space.

We hear the term, 'And then they just switched on,' and do not take it literally when we really should.

On the way home, we stop at the Waggon & Horses pub, which has recently reopened under the auspices of our friend Simon, formerly the landlord of the Aspinall Arms, where Matt and I held the inaugural Cloudspotting in the beer garden. Now, Simon has two places in Clitheroe; the Ale House is a small bar in the centre of town, whereas the Waggon & Horses is a larger traditional-style pub just outside the centre. Lamont and I attempt to order two pints of Gorilla's Fist before Simon informs the new and bemused bar tender that we are in fact taking the piss, and then with a pint each of Blonde Witch in our hands, we go for a game of darts, both needing the practise ahead of our annual weekend away in Barras.

For sixteen years, a group of us have been booking a big house and engaging in a decathlon of events known as Majors. The blue-ribbon event is the 501 darts, for which each contestant has their own stage name and accompanying walk-on music. Obviously, I am the Terminal Chancer, and my song is A Shot in the Dark by Henri Mancini. In 2021, I won both the catapult target shooting and the darts 501, and since the place we stayed even had a small trout lake, I had them all catching fish on the fly by the time we left.

In the early years of this tradition, it was a crazy, heavy weekend, but as we age it's getting lighter and more mellow, if you get my drift. The essence remains the same, though: friendship, music, needle and lots of laughter. The glamour event is Staying the Distance, Friday night to Monday morning; the Sunday club are the elite of the elite, and I am proud to be a stoic founding member. Our friend, the bow-legged Al True, usually scuttles out early on the Saturday, a move which is roundly frowned upon. His tired old bones just can't take it anymore; he's liable to nod off while you're in the middle of talking to him. If he was a horse, he'd be shot (more than once).

There's only ever been one 180 recorded in the long, prestigious history of the Majors, so Lamont and I are playing darts. Tentatively, I enquire if my tickled salmon counts, prompting him to spit his pint out.

That's a no, then.

Clearing his throat, he asks, 'Did you hear about Barry?'

'Who, Leatherhead?' I say, spinning a full three-sixty, panicked in case he's just walked in, like a storm cloud of doom.

'Yeah,' Lamont nods, 'he's dead. His dog murdered him.'

'What!' I exclaim. 'How?'

'They'd been for a walk, and then Barry and the dog jump back into his van. He starts the engine, but notices that his offside wing mirror is folded in, so he gets out and walks around the front to fix it – that's when the mutt takes its chance and pounces on the gear stick. The van lurches forward, banjoing Happy Barry right under. Killed instantly. One of his hair plugs was recovered from under the windscreen wiper. At first, they thought it was a tape worm. The dog had lived with the dull bastard for seven years, imagine that. I bet the poor thing needed counselling.'

'It should get a medal for endurance,' I say, scoring twenty-six yet again.

'You know the painting by Edvard Munch, the Scream? That was a response to Barry Leatherhead plodding up the riverbank to ask, "Is there owt, doing? I bet there isn't." He was the silent assassin on any forum or social media page, stitching together a dystopian image of the river, like a depressing patchwork Frankenstein – the collapsed star that forms a black hole. That poor dog cracked. It must have been biding its time for years, waiting until Baz was at his most vulnerable. I wonder how many failed and aborted attempts the hound had been through, probably more than the CIA tried with Castro.' Lamont throws a convincing sixty before adding, 'The dog has been adopted by somebody in the Cayman Islands.'

What a result. I suppose fortune does favour the brave.

For the next two hours, we play bad darts and discuss potential book sales and the merits of Planet Rod Licence.

Between 2020 and 2021, the EA (Environment Agency) nobly sold over 23,388 migratory salmon and sea trout licences in England and Wales. With each licence costing the lucky punter £82, this generated a tidy sum of £1,917,816, and of those plucky 23,388, most blanked, as only 5,815 salmon were caught. Let's say, for argument's sake, that the 5,815 lucky anglers all got one each, that leaves 17,573 blanking. Happily, 5,535 caught fish were released and 280 killed, giving us a catch and release rate of 95%. Now, as I'm sure you're all aware, the vast majority of licence holders will also be paid-up members of at least one local club, meaning they will at some point do a bit of work on the river, and in most cases, the clubs will be part of a local river trust, which involves paying a fee that goes towards all the incredible work they do. Naturally, the clubs I pay into are part of the Ribble Trust.

In addition to contributing towards the upkeep of our precious waters, each club is also asked to report on bird counts, poaching, pollution incidents, extraction, kick sampling and invertebrate counts. We care, deeply, so for just £82 annually, we get the privilege of doing the EA's job for them. We provide all that data and free labour on an ongoing basis. There isn't a walking tax, a wild swimming tax, a climbing tax, a mountain-biking tax or a canoeing tax. Why are we anglers the only ones forced to chip in? Maybe ask the private water companies for the £2m instead? After all, they bank billions in profits from our water, and surely clean waterways and rivers are in the national interest.

What's more important than clean water?

So, why don't they just get shut, scrap it and give us anglers a break? If the only reason the licence fee is £82 is because we can take a fish then, personally, I'd be more than happy to go full catch-and-release. It has to be in our collective best interest to give it a go for ten years and then review, hasn't it? Just have a free licence that must be registered in order for the EA to gather the data they need.

There's one more really annoying thing about the 23,000 licence buyers. Why haven't they all bought a sodding book from me? Is it time to get together and petition the EA to force them to buy all the sorry blankers one of my books by way of compensation, as a gesture of goodwill? Blank three seasons in a row, and they snap your rods in front of you and order you to buy a large abstract painting of mine. Actually, what our sport really needs is for Lamont to infiltrate the EA and bring it down from within, utilising his cunning interview techniques to slither his way to the top.

Food for thought.

Tuesday evening, 31st January 2023. Sitting in my kitchen, listening to Joy Lovejoy singing In Orbit, writing the end of Anarchy Pie. Since February 2021, our worlds have been turned upside down in a new cyclone of fear. Many didn't make it, and though we carry the grief with us as we go about our lives, at least we're still here. Thus, my head remains full of hopeful sparkling butterflies; brighter days are surely around the corner.

Keep casting, and keep on keeping on.

I've called my family – Francis, fourteen; Rose, eleven; and Ams, fifty-one – into the kitchen. They've got their arms around me as I type this, what a privilege! They know how much it means to me; my dream is that you have enjoyed the read and smiled. Now, there's only one more thing to do.

Removing Nina Simone's incredible and amazing 45" single Ain't Got No, I Got Life from its sleeve, I place it on the slip mat and carefully lower the needle. After a reassuringly quiet crackle, Miss Simone begins as Ams pours me a glass of red,

while Rose and I proceed to dance and sing.
    Keep dancing.

Cut.
Playhappy,
Boo

Printed in Great Britain
by Amazon

31064237R00085